Dropshipping in 2019 :

The Latest Strategies to Start an Ecommerce on Shopify / Ebay, Step By Step Guide on How to Make Passive Income and Make Money Online from Home

© Copyright 2019 by Jack Gary

All rights reserved.

This Book is written with the sole purpose of providing relevant information on a specific topic for which every reasonable effort has been made to ensure that it is both accurate and reasonable. Nevertheless, by purchasing this Book, you consent to the fact that the author, as well as the publisher, are in no way experts on the topics contained herein, regardless of any claims as such that may be made within. As such, any suggestions or recommendations that are made within are done so purely for entertainment value. It is recommended that you always consult a professional prior to undertaking any of the advice or techniques discussed within.

This is a legally binding declaration that is considered both valid and fair by both the Committee of Publishers Association and the American Bar Association and should be considered as legally binding within the United States.

The reproduction, transmission, and duplication of any of the content found herein, including any specific or extended information will be done as an illegal act regardless of the end form the information ultimately takes. This includes copied versions of the work, both physical, digital and audio unless express consent of the Publisher is provided beforehand. Any additional rights reserved.

Furthermore, the information that can be found within the pages described forthwith shall be considered both accurate and truthful when it comes to the recounting of facts. As such, any use, correct or incorrect, of the provided information will render the Publisher free of responsibility as to the actions taken outside of their direct purview. Regardless, there are zero scenarios where the original author or the Publisher can be deemed liable in any fashion for any damages or hardships that may result from any of the information discussed herein.

Additionally, the information in the following pages is intended only for informational purposes and should thus be thought of as universal. As befitting its nature, it is presented without assurance regarding its prolonged validity or interim quality. Trademarks that are mentioned are done without written consent and can in no way be considered an endorsement from the trademark holder.

Table of Contents

Introduction 6
Chapter 1: The Power of Dropshipping............ 12
Chapter 2: Building Your Dropshipping Website... 16
Chapter 3: The Good, The Bad, and The Ugly: How Much Money Will I Need to Start My Business? 33

    The Successful Dropshipping Mindset 33
    Branding 40
    The Downright Ugly 49
    Another Ugly Truth 51
    Answers to The Tough Questions................. 53

Chapter 4: Supplying and Fulfilling: How It All Works 57
    Best Practices.. 63

Chapter 5: The Riches Are in the Niches: Choosing the Products You Will Sell 67
Chapter 6: Supplier and Inventory 101............ 84
Chapter 7: Easy Customer Service 91

    Product Returns 101 91
    Shipping Issues... 93
    Customer Service Best Practices 98

Chapter 8: Marketing Your Dropshipping Business.. 103

Chapter 9: How to Scale Your Business......... 128
Chapter 10: Other Considerations 131

    The Bank Account Issue 145
    Don't Forget..147

Conclusion..151

    Quick Guide to Get Started 154
    Pros and Cons..155
    Why People Fail..157

Introduction

An unknown wise person once said, 'The dream is free, but the hustle is sold separately." The road to becoming an entrepreneur is not easy. For many who want to embark upon the entrepreneur lifestyle, they have no problem thinking about their lofty goals of fame and fortune. Yet, in order to reach their goals, they have to put in the work, or the hustle. This path is even more difficult if you shouldmake it in the dropshipping business. While it may be difficult to achieve success, it is not impossible. Many people have started thriving dropshipping businesses. These brands did not start off being successful. They built their way to the top from the bottom. If you are interested in starting a dropshipping business, you too can start and build your way to the top of the success ladder.

This book is all about helping you start your dropshipping business. All dropshipping businesses have common pieces that are needed to be successful. The most important common denominator among all these brands is the hard work that the founders put in to jumpstart their company's success. Do not take the words 'hard work' lightly. To be successful, you will be required to put in lots of hard work. Hard work means sleepless nights, days with no money, obstacles that you will feel like you cannot overcome, even debt and stress. Hard work can mean that your friends and family do not understand why you are staying up at all hours of the night to make your dream come true instead of hanging out with them. Hard work means that you may have to isolate yourself for a time until you meet your business goals. Hard work means that you may be alone. However, the end goal is worth it, and the owners of some of the most successful dropshipping companies will agree.

So why would somebody want to leave the comfortable life of working a regular, stable, nine-to-five job and embark upon the unstable, wild world of owning your own business? There are many reasons. The thrill of being your own boss is the first reason. Many people love to do what they want to do, when they want to do it. When you are your own boss, you do not have to worry about others telling you what to do. You are the one that gets to tell others what to do, and they HAVE to listen to you. When you are an entrepreneur, you have the joy of being able to take what you see in your mind and make it a reality. There is an unspeakable rush when you see others buying from you.

Another major reason becoming a dropshipper is attractive is because you are paid what you are worth. If you were working a traditional job, you would be paid an hourly rate, oftentimes wishing that you were making more money. However, the amount of money you can make from owning your own business is astronomically higher compared to working for someone else. The work to pay ratio when you are an entrepreneur is definitely better. That work to pay ratio is limitless, especially if your business is successful. When you own your own business, someone else does not become rich off of your hard work. When you own your own business, you do not have to dread going to work every day, knowing that someone is living a comfortable lifestyle from your hard work. As a business owner, you, and only you are the beneficiary of all of your hard work. You determine what other people make, whether they are employees or freelancers because you are in charge. If you want to cut everyone's pay, you can. If you want to give everyone a raise, you can. You are the boss and what you say GOES. This book will help you begin the journey towards owning your own business and becoming the boss you are destined to be.

For some who already has capital saved up, they are ready to jump head into starting dropshipping. For others, they may have to work while building their dropshipping on the side or use a different model that does not require any money upfront. The great thing about either method is that you are taking action. That's the most important thing to take away from this book. If you do not remember anything else, remember this. The sooner you start, the sooner you will be able to have the dropshipping business of your dreams. You do not have to know everything up front. You do not have to wait until everything is perfect. Many people waste time biting their fingernails and stressing over what moves to make. Approach your business as a marathon. It is not a sprint. You have to get started in order to reach the end. You also need to be flexible with change because as a business owner, things in the business world change all the time. Know that your business idea and business methods are going to change many times until you get comfortable. The best way to get comfortable is to start.

The following chapters will help you start. They will discuss everything you need to know to start your dream company. In Chapter 1, you will learn what makes dropshipping such a powerful business model. In Chapter 2, you learn all about the different options to build your dropshipping website. We will explore questions that you should ask yourself in Chapter 3. Chapter 4 is all about the supply and fulfillment cycle when you are a dropshipper. Chapter 5 helps you figure out which type of product to sell by focusing on niches. Chapter 6 will help you figure out how to find your supplier and manage your inventory. In chapter 7, an easy way to handle your customers will be given, and in chapter 8, attention will be given to the different marketing tools you can use to market your business. In chapter 9, different methods on how to scale your business will be given, and we will end with other considerations to have in mind as you begin your dropshipping business.

The information provided can feel overwhelming, but it is important to note that by the time you finish, you will have everything you need to start your business. Just take everything step-by-step, and you will be moving towards your goals in no time. Be mindful that there are lots of things that you may have to do on your own. There are lots of things to research. (Remember, it takes hard work.) The more you research in, the more you connect with people who are doing what you want to do, the easier your journey will be. Always be open to learning more because you have to be adaptable as a business owner if you're going to be successful. There is no way around it. However, if you are determined to succeed, you will be able to overcome any challenges that you may face. Stay positive and keep going. Think of failure as a positive thing. You will only know what works once you fail. So fail a lot and learn a lot.

There are plenty of books on this subject on the market, thanks again for choosing this one! Every effort was made to ensure it is full of as much useful information as possible. Please enjoy!

Chapter 1: The Power of Dropshipping

This chapter will explore what dropshipping is in more detail, and why it is such a powerful business model to have. To begin, we will explore what dropshipping is. Dropshipping is essentially creating a store and selling products on that store, but instead of housing the product yourself, you use a third-party business to send the product to the customer for you. You do not touch the product. Instead, you simply place the order and keep the profits. In other words, the dropshipping model focuses on you managing the order process, rather than creating and selling your product by leveraging the products of other businesses.

A simple breakdown of the dropshipping process would look like this.
   1. Researching a product and finding a dropship supplier, creating your website and marketing, eventually a customer will place an order on your website. You collect the money from the sale and your customer's order details.

2. Using the customer's information, you then send the order quantity and customer shipping details to the supplier. You pay the supplier the agreed upon price for the product and keep the difference.
3. Your dropship supplier will then fulfill the order and send it to the customer like the order is coming from your business. You never have to touch the product. Some suppliers will also include personalized tags at an extra cost to customize the product to your business.
4. Your customer gets the order, is happy, and you make more sales!

It's a simple process, which is effective and easy, and a favorite of many people to do. Dropshipping has been around and does not look like it will be going away anytime soon. However, the dropshipping market has become more competitive because so many people are attracted to the ease of entry.

Dropshipping is an attractive, online business model for a few reasons.

- Low, start-up costs – You don't have to spend a lot of money, up front. You can get started for less than $20 and even a smaller amount if you have graphic design skills or know someone who can create a website for you.
- No hassle inventory – As a dropshipper, you don't have to worry about inventory at all. You don't have to worry about dealing with inventory being stored in a spare room or garage at your house. You don't have to worry about it at all. Since you are not dealing with inventory, you don't have to have a lot of capital in order to get started.
- It's flexible to do anywhere. – Dropshipping is amazing because you are location-independent. As long as you have an internet connection, you can operate your store. This

model is so fun because you can be on the beach and run your store at any time that you'd like.
- Overall, low barrier to entry – If you have time to do research and a determination to succeed, you don't have to worry about whether you have background knowledge or not. You can learn how it works, set up your store and begin dropshipping.
- Lots of supports – Because dropshipping is a popular online business model, there are so many resources that you can draw information from if you have questions. You can learn from the success of others and the failures of others to improve your business. Whatever info you should find about dropshipping, you can find a resource to help you find it.

Dropshipping has been around for years because it can be such a lucrative business model. Understanding how dropshipping works is the first step in becoming a dropshipper. Now that you understand how it works, we can now focus on how to set up your dropshipping website, which will be the subject of the next chapter.

Chapter 2: Building Your Dropshipping Website

The next important aspect of your dropshipping business that you should to consider is your website. Your website is an important aspect in bringing people to you. There are a few different ways to help bring your website to life. You also want to make sure that your website ties into your branding (More will be given on branding in the next chapter.) If you have certain colors in your logo, you want your website to reflect those colors as well. You should make sure that you are using a similar font on your website that's in your logo. That way you have a consistent branding message no matter where they see an asset advertising your business. The types of options you use for your website depend upon your budget and your technical skill. It also depends on how much time you have and what type of tools you should take advantage of. This chapter is all about ways to design your website. We will discuss a few different ways to create your website, including Shopify, Big Cartel, WordPress, and hiring a graphic designer to build your website.

One of the most popular ways to create your business's website is to use Shopify. Shopify is highly recommended because many people already use it, and they have many great back-office tools. Shopify also easily connects to many print-on-demand services easily. Shopify has a free two-week trial that you can use, but in order to actually sell on your website, you will need to pay at least the minimum pricing to have access to the selling features. Using Shopify is a very popular option. Many successful companies use Shopify. There is a lot of support from the Shopify website itself, along with Shopify communities, blogs, and tutorials about how to use Shopify. Therefore, if you go with this option, you will not fail for lack of information.

At this time, Shopify has three different tiers. The first year is the basic teir, and it cost $29 a month. The next tier is $79 a month, and the highest tier is $229 dollars a month. Every Shopify tier allows you to create discount codes and sell unlimited products on your website. It also gives you a way to email people if they abandon their cart, and it protects your website from hackers with an SSL certificate. This certificate is needed to protect the credit card information of people that buy your products. The higher Shopify tier you purchase, the more bells and whistles you have access to.

Shopify has a payment system built in that they charge you to use. It is built in so you should adjust your pricing to account for their processing charges. If you are using the most basic tier of Shopify, anytime you make a sell, you pay 2.9% plus 30 cents if the customer is using an online credit card. If you have the first tier, and the customer is paying in person, then you only pay they only pay 2.7% of the price. If the customer is using any other payment method, there is a 2% charge. If you are using the second Shopify tier, anytime you make a sale online, you pay 2.6% plus 30 cents if they are using an online credit card. If you are using the second Shopify tier, you only pay 2.5% plus 30 cents if the customer is using a credit card in person, but if they are using any other payment method, then there is a 1% charge. If you are using the third Shopify tier anytime you make a sale online you pay 2.4% plus 30 cents if they are using an online credit card. If they are using an in-person credit card, they only pay 2.74%, and if they are using any other payment method is a 0.5% charge. With all the tiers, you have the ability to print shipping levels which makes your order fulfillment easier. Shopify is relatively easy to use, and it has a lot of bells and whistles in the backdrop. If you ever want to customize your Shopify website, you can either buy a theme or use the free themes that they have to customize your website.

If you shouldbuy a domain name to represent your business, you can use your Shopify store with that domain name. Shopify also has 24/7 hour support for any questions you may have, which is a major perk. If you shouldsell just on your social media platforms, without having a Shopify website, you could consider Shopify Lite. This does not give you the option to create your own Shopify store, but it is a lot cheaper than the basic plan, and it starts off at $9 a month. Depending on what country you are in determines how you will be paid. You can connect your PayPal or your bank account to Shopify. And for US customers, every two days Shopify will put your profits into your bank account or PayPal account. You also need to be aware that the fees will be taken out of your payments before it is deposited into your account.

Anytime you are setting up an online presence to take payments; you have to be mindful of the fees that you may be charged. Some e-commerce websites charge a fee just to use their payment processing. Payment processing is important because it is a secure way to accept payments, and you do not have to worry about setting a secure way to process money on your own which can be a strenuous process. So you have to be aware of the fees that your e-commerce processing may charge. For example, if they are using a payment processor like PayPal or Stripe, they will take a fee of the cost and the website will take the processing fee, too. These fees are minimal, but they can still add up. You should also make sure that the payment processor or the e-commerce site you are using does not have any minimum processing requirements. Some require that you make a certain amount of sales every month, or they will charge you a fee. When examining the site that you should use to set up your business, be mindful of that. In order to make the most money, you should make sure that you have the most options for your customer to make a payment with, too. Not everyone has PayPal, not everyone has Stripe, and not everyone has a Visa. If you have the majority of payment options, then you will be okay.

You also want to think if you are going to accept cashier's checks or personal checks. Most payment processors are also safeguarding you against fraud, so you do not have to worry about accepting payments from fraudulent credit cards. If you want to find any extra designers for hire in setting up your Shopify store, there is a marketplace for you to get assistance.

It is also rather easy to connect print-on-demand websites to Shopify. After you create your Shopify store, there is a place for you to select apps to connect to your Shopify in the back office. A popular print-on-demand app to use is called Printful. To connect it, you would need to login to Shopify. Then select the Apps option. When you select the apps, you will select the Printful app and connect your store to Printful. You will be required to submit your billing information, which you should do at that time. Next, you shouldmake sure that the products you are selling on Printful are already listed in your Shopify store. If they are already listed, that's perfect. Anytime you are adding a product, remember that a variant is the same product, but just a different version of the product. For example, shirt sizes are variants of a certain shirt. Or the color of the shirt is a different variant. So when you create your products make sure that you have all the necessary variants listed. Once your products are created, then you will go to your Printful app in your Printful account. In the back surface of Printful, you go to the store and then click on products. At this point, your Shopify products should show up in the Printful interface.

You can then select the products from your Shopify store that you shouldbe fulfilled by Printful. You will be asked about the information and the picture of the product. Once that information is added, you are finished. Once set up, any item that is on your Shopify is now fulfilled by Printful. Other print-on-demand apps that you can use with Shopify are Teelaunch, Gooten, Pillow Profits, Print Aura, and Viralstyle. The good thing about Shopify is that new apps are being added daily that allows you to fulfill print-on-demand products. Most of these apps have a similar process to Printful that require you to add the app to your Shopify store. Shopify is a robust first choice that many people choose to use, and with good reason.

Another option that you can use for your print-on-demand store is Big Cartel. Printful also connects to

Big Cartel in the back end. Big Cartel is an e-commerce website that was made with artists and creative people in mind. Their price is not quite as expensive as Shopify. Their pricing tiers start off a little bit cheaper than Shopify; Big Cartel does have a limit on how many products you can upload to the site. Whereas Shopify has unlimited products no matter which tier you purchase, Big Cartel's first tier is free, but it only consists of 5 products. When you start selling more than five products, then you have to pay. The next level on Big Cartel of 25 products costs $9.99 a month; to sell a hundred products, it costs $19.99 a month; to sell 300 products, it costs $29.99 Big Cartel does not take a portion of your payments for processing, but they have a limited number of payment options they accept. They only accept Stripe and PayPal as payments. So you will only be responsible for the fees that PayPal and Stripe require. It is 2.75% for Stripe and 2.9% + $0.30 for PayPal. Shopify also has many integrations that you can use compared to Big Cartel. Big Cartel also has standard themes, but you can change the themes for free as well.

The next way to create your website is to use WordPress. WordPress is a free software you can use to create your website. There are lots of free integrations you can use to customize your website, such as themes. You can choose a free three or buy premium things to give your store the look you want. Once you have your WordPress account created, you will then need to use a plug-in that allows your WordPress site to take payments. A popular plug-in that's free and many people use is called WooCommerce. While WooCommerce is free to customize the website, you have to pay for more plug-ins. If you shouldaccept lots of payments other than the Stripe and PayPal that comes with WooCommerce, you can add other plug-ins like authorize.net for $79 at the time of this writing. However, keep in mind that PayPal accepts all types of credit cards. You can also accept, Square and Amazon payments too when using WooCommerce.

However, the tricky part with creating a WordPress site is to always make sure it is up to date to prevent hacks. Also, unlike an e-commerce site like Big Cartel or Shopify, you will need to purchase an SSL certificate in order to accept payments. An SSL certificate secures your site so it can accept payments. You can also add extra plug-ins for security on your website. Unlike Big Cartel and Shopify, you will have to be diligent in making sure the security on your site is up-to-date if you go the WordPress option. However, it is a much cheaper option because you are not paying a monthly fee. You also want to have a backup of your site and use strong passwords, so security can be top notch. Some people do not want to deal with the security issues that could potentially happen, so they avoid using WordPress. But just like Big Cartel and Shopify, if you go the WordPress option, you can have your own domain name. Making sure that your domain and hosting is reputable is another major way to protect security. However, if you do not mind the challenge, WordPress has lots of forums where you can learn information. Their support isn't as friendly for people who are not tech-savvy. You have to find solutions on your own, so it is a very DIY approach.

A quick note about domain names: a domain name is just the name of your website. You can purchase one from a domain name seller or hosting seller. A domain name is what allows your domain name to come on the internet. Then to turn it in a show it will show up when people visit your domain name is called hosting. Sites like Big Cartel or Shopify already pay for hosting, so you just point the sites to your domain name. This means that when your domain name is typed in it will go straight to your Shopify or Big Cartel store instead of the longer name that you get when you sign up for free. Some people like to have a matching domain name with their brand without the Shopify or Big Cartel details in their domain name. For others, they want to save money, so they keep the name that Shopify or Big Cartel gives them when they open their store. If possible, you will want to choose a '.com'. Most people view this type of website as legitimate once they visit, and it helps people to find your website easier. If there is not a domain name with the '.com.' option available, other popular names include '.info,' '.site', '.review', or '.co'. There are new domain names everyday. When you are checking for domain names, also be aware of the renewal charge. Every time you buy a domain name you have to renew the domain name yearly. This renewal charge allows you to maintain ownership of the domain name. If you do not pay the renewal charge, you no longer own the website. The renewal price will be listed so make sure it is a price that you can afford. Sometimes it is cheap to buy the domain name, but the renewal price can be a lot of money. You will also want to make sure the domain comes with some type of protection like 'Whoisguard' which protects your personal information. When you register your domain name without 'Whoisguard' protection when people look up the website they can see your personal details that you included in the purchase of the website, so you should protect yourself if you can. Most companies include this type of protection for free, and you renew it for a few bucks the following year when you renew your site.

It is totally up to you which option you think is best. However, if you do build a site from scratch, you have to power that website to turn it on by buying a hosting package. There are certain different hosting packages that help your company handle the volume that you may receive. Popular hosting websites to visit are Bluehost, Namecheap, or even Go Daddy. All three approaches also have a way for you to add fulfillment apps to make sure that when people play their orders, you can track them and make sure that they are being fulfilled. They are also ways to incorporate shipping apps into your end; you can cut down the shipping process. These apps allow you to print labels for the products that people order, so you just have to package your product and take it to the store. However, if you want to customize everything for your site, there is another way.

The next way isif you have a lot of money and you do not mind customizing your site, is to build a site from scratch. You will hire a graphic designer and a coder and let them design everything. They will build the site from scratch using code. If you have a graphic designer who can code, that's even better. This method can be expensive, but it lets you have all of the features that you want on your website. The most difficult part will be to find a designer that can design the site according to your specifications. Of course, you should look at inside job boards like freelancer or fiverr.com or upwork.com to see if you can find the designer. You can also find designers that will use WordPress to design a website for you.

You just want to make sure that you guys have some type of documentation and place for confidentiality reasons and make sure you have great communication in your working relationship. Some people like to accept your payment, without doing your work. So make sure that you have specific guidelines about when they are getting paid. This option is definitely for more advanced people, and you may spend more money up front, but in the long term, it may help you save more money if your site becomes very popular and you start having higher volume. The more places you are, the more chances you have to make more money. So you want also to consider being on sites like Zazzle, Poshmark, Etsy, eBay, and Amazon. These sites have a fee per sale model. There are many different options you can use to sell your products. You just have to think about your short-term and long-term goals in order to choose the one that fits the idea that you are trying to do. These sites have a built-in market that can help with selling your product, but you have to be aware of the fees they charge when a customer buys from you. You also want to consider how these sites handle shipping. For ease of shipping, Poshmark is a favorite, to begin with, especially if you are selling clothing since you don't have to worry about weighing your items. It's a simple, flat rate. More attention will be given to supplying and fulfilling orders later in the book.

Every year you should evaluate your website. As you make more money, you may even consider hiring a business coach to look at your website, especially one that specializes in e-commerce. A business coach can point out toareas of opportunity to improve sales just based on your website. They can help you find where you need to create a sense of urgency that will increase sales. They will also know which plug-ins you can add that will improve the overall customer's purchase when they come to your website. They may be expensive, so this is a step you should take when you definitely have more money. If you have enough money upfront, do not be afraid to invest in yourself. They can definitely help.

When your website is created, do not forget to have a frequently asked questions page to answer questions about shipping and other pressing issues. As a dropshipper, you should have this information highlighted so if people ever have questions or want to dispute something, you can point to the policy on the website as a clear indication of your dropshipping policy. Also, make sure you have a way for people to contact you as well. This is information that people want to know. If they are able to easily look on your website and find it, it will save you a lot of time.

The first service is called print on demand, and it works like this. First, you upload a graphic design to a print on demand site and set the design up on different products like shirts, sweatshirts, mugs posters, or whatever products the print on demand site offers. Then you position the design on the products just how you want. And then choose to put the products on sale. Second, you can post the design to your company's website. Third, when somebody orders your print on demand piece, the print-on-demand company will receive the customer's information, the size they want, their address, and company, and will produce the product and ship the order for you. You will not have to do anything, except upload your design and position it on the products. The print-on-demand company fulfills the order, and this method is completely passive. Some print-on-demand companies offer customized features, like customized tags so you can brand your business better.

The pros of this method are that you do not have to order a lot of items upfront and you can let them handle fulfilling all the orders. The cons to print on demand are the royalties you receive and the restriction on your design placements and blank items you can use. The print-on-demand company takes a portion of everything that you sell and send you the royalties. Another advantage with this method is that you do not have to have your own site, you can just use their site to sell your items. Another con is that you are limited to the types of designs that they have on their sites. Overall, this is a much lower risk because you do not have to order large quantities of product and worry about putting them in a warehouse! There are no minimum orders and the company only prints what the customer wants so you do not have the risk of having extra, unwanted inventory. Popular print-on-demand sites are services like Printful, Zazzle, Printify, or Print Aura to name a few. More print-on-demand services are being started every day with each company having differing offerings. You can take your designs and put them on various blank items like shirts, sweatshirt, and other options like mugs. Really, the options are endless. So you just have to research and see which company offers the print-on-demand selection that you prefer.

Chapter 3: The Good, The Bad, and The Ugly: How Much Money Will I Need to Start My Business?

This chapter will give you the good, the bad, and the ugly about dropshipping. While dropshipping is an excellent way to make money, there are some difficulties you may face. This chapter will help paint the overall picture to help you understand the dropshipping method more before you dive in. This chapter is especially important to read so you can figure out how to set yourself apart from your competition. This starts with your mindset which will be the subject of the next section.

The Successful Dropshipping Mindset

Sure, having your own business sounds good, but those who want to be successful as an online business owner must have a certain mindset. If you don't have this mindset, then you won't be able to make it. The mindset of a successful online business owner consists of four pillars.

1. The first pillar is that you must be committed to hard work. Some may even call you a workaholic and rightfully so. Business owners will put as much time as they need into their business. Successful business owners put in a lot of work. Sometimes they put in a lot of work before they even see results. This is not normal. Some people are afraid of hard work. They are always looking for the shortcuts in life to do the least amount of work possible. Business owners do the exact opposite. They understand that hard work is necessary to achieve their dreams. They approach their journey to business ownership with the expectation that they are going to work hard. The hard work does not deter them, but rather the ability to not reach their dreams is more important than hard work. It's this obsessive commitment to hard work that drives business owners, and it is at the core of being one.

2. The next pillar of the business owner's mindset is the willingness to invest money in their business. Business owners know that to make a business run you have to invest money.

Oftentimes, with limited resources, they find themselves investing their own money. They know how to save their money to help them make it through the lean times. They have the discipline to put their money back into their business instead of spending it. They use the money that they make to work for them. They are quick to learn and use the info to make more money.

On the other hand, investing money in their business can also be a business owner's downfall. If a business owner is investing too much money into a sinking ship, they are not being smart. However, successful business owners know when it's smart to stop investing their money, but they are not afraid to spend it. Even if they spend too much money into their business, they are able to quickly make adjustments in the best interest of their business.

3. The next important pillar of being a business owner is knowing how to focus their time wisely. Working hard is important, but if you

work hard on things that do not matter to your business, then your work is pointless. Successful business owners know how to focus on the most important activities that help their businesses grow. They focus on the task that brings in money and outsource the rest. (More information about outsourcing will be given later in the book.) Once they figure out what activities make the most money for their business, they spend time on those tasks.

Successful business owners are master time management practitioners. It's easy to get sucked into the vortex of trying to do everything for your business. Successful business owners do the opposite. They focus on the most important things so they can have a well-rounded lifestyle. This commitment to focus and to manage their time allows them to stay on the business path longer than those business owners who try to do everything and find themselves being burned out.

4. The last important thing that successful business owners know how to do is be objective. Most people have a bias to their abilities and their efforts. This blind bias makes them take bad decision after bad decision, especially when it comes to their business babies. Business owners are objective about their expectations and goals when it comes to their business. They are able to see if what they're doing is working and don't get emotional about it. They can handle feedback constructively, but they are their most constructive critic. They take the feelings out of their business and look at the data to see if it supports what they are trying to do. If what they see supports their expectations and goals then they continue to do those actions. However, if their expectations and those are not being met, business owners do not feel bad about taking a new path to reach those goals or modifying their expectations and reality. Unfortunately, many people have certain expectations about their business, but once they start working, they realize that those expectations don't correlate in the real world.

People love to think about business but are shocked what happens when they actually do business.

Business owners are not so committed to their ideas that they are not able to change. They understand that the business is constantly changing, and they don't take the changes that their business may show them personally. This ability to be objective helps them find the proper resources that will help their business to succeed. If they feel they are too close to the business, they don't mind asking mentors or hiring business coaches to be objective with them. Successful business owners know that being objective is the only way that their business can survive, and they seek out best information to help them measure their business against so they can survive long-term.

In conclusion, being a business owner is a dream that many have, but not many are willing to work for it. Having a successful business is not just selling your company for millions of bucks. Having a successful business means a commitment to excellence and lots of hard work reeling to meet your business's goals and expectations. In order to be a true business owner, you must have a foundation on a mindset consisting of four pillars. The first is a love for hard work; the second is a commitment to investing money in your business; the third is knowing how to focus on the money-making task of your business, and the fourth pillar is knowing how to be objective.

Business ownership is very rewarding, but there is hard work that goes into it. If you are willing to make the commitment, then you're going to have a lot of fun. If you're not sold on the hard work that it takes to be successful, then stop reading now. However, if you're up to the challenge, keep reading. Because drop shipping has become so popular, you have to brand your business well, which will be the subject of this next section, and one of the best places to begin.

Branding

Branding is a big decision. Every dropshipper has to decide what they want their brand to be. Your brand has to be exciting, unique, and fit into your ideals. Your brand is important because it separates you from other companies. Some people have very strict methodologies about what type of brand name is most successful for a dropshipping company. Some people have a strict list of do's and don'ts. However, I believe the proper branding for your company is whatever you truly feel you want to do. It is not as hard as you think. The branding should speak to the product that you are selling. Many people have ideas for brands, but they are not sure about how to bring the idea to life. If you have purchased this book, then I'm sure you have already thought of an idea for a brand. This chapter will help you refine the branding idea that you already have or help you create a brand if you do not have one already. Initially, you should start off with strong branding because the brand will be associated with your business for a very long time. The branding consists of the physical assets such as the colors and physical imaging of your branding, like your logo. Your brand is also abstract as it is the story behind your company. Two important components help determine what your branding will be. The first component is the brand concept or the idea for your business. The next component important to your brand is going to be your target market.

The idea behind your business is the brand concept. Simply put, the brand concept is about what your brand represents. To help form your brand concept, you should ask yourself a few important questions.

- When people see your brand, what ideas do you want them to associate with your brand? - Do you want them to think of youthfulness or maturity? Do you want them to think of free-spirited people or business-minded people? What other ideas do you want them to think about when they hear your brand's name or see your brand's imaging. There is no right or wrong answer to this. It is simply what you want your brand to be.
- What is your mission statement? - You may think a mission statement is a broad, detailed story, but it is simply what you want your company to do or be. What kind of goals do you want to reach with your company? Do you want to be the top grossing baby line company

in the world or would you like to be the most successful luggage company in the world? Do you want to help stop poverty with a portion of your sales? Whatever your goal is for your company that is what your mission statement should be.

- What is your brand story? - Your brand story is different from your mission statement; although they may share some overlap. The brand story talks about the origins of your company, whereas the mission talks about the goals of your company. You can incorporate your origin story or the initial idea that inspired you to start your company. People connect to a brand story because they are able to see themselves in the brand. Make sure that the brand story is written in a way that's relatable and truthful. It is a foundational aspect of your business.

- What colors do you want to represent your brand question? - Choosing the colors of your brand is very important. If your brand has a calm vibe, then you most likely will want a calm color to represent your brand. A fiery color like orange and red may not be ideal, but a cool color like blue or light green may be more ideal. However, there is no hard-and-fast rule for the colors that you choose. Your brand makes the color. Do not stress if your colors are like another business because there are only so many colors in the world, so a few businesses are bound to use the same kind. However, make sure that your colors represent your brand in a way that it is not used by another brand. That's where your brand story in your mission statement comes into play.

- What logo would you like to represent your brand? - Some people like to just use logos or initials to represent their brand. The type of font used in the logo is also part of the brand. There are lots of different companies that can help you develop your brand. A popular website to use is fiverr.com. The designers there will ask you questions, and you can brainstorm with them to find your brand for cheap. Other people like to use free logos and add their own fonts with a website like Canva, which is another low-cost option.

Once you have your initial branding down, you will then want to think about your target market. They may influence your branding efforts as well. A great activity to do when trying to figure out who your target market is to create three brand identities of the people who will buy your product. This helps you to learn more about your customers, and find a brand that will appeal to them. It is important to know multiple types of customers you are targeting because different target markets will be attracted to your business for different reasons. Knowing your target audience may help you prevent a no-no. For example, if you have a vegan company, you may not want to have a bloody cow as your logo. Thinking about your customer can help you come up with cool ideas and ways that you can connect to them. When trying to figure out who your target market is going to be, you should do your research. You may realize that your idea may not work after you do research. However, these three brand identities will help you research further and find out more about your customer. It is important to note that when you begin, you will learn more about your customers. As the information comes in about who is buying your product, do not be afraid to adjust some of your branding efforts at the point.

When you think about the brand identities here are a few questions that you can ask.

- Where is your customer from? What country or continent are they from? What city in that country are they from?
- How old is your target demographic? Try to narrow this down as much as possible. Have one major segment and then another major segment for two major target demographics.
- Will your product solve a certain problem for them? Is your target demographic unable to find styles that work for them that your style will address?
- Does your product represent a certain ideal for them? Is your product brand the most expensive form of product that they can ever afford? Is it an urban style?
- Where does your customer stay most of the time when they are on the internet? Are they browsing social media or are they on news websites?
- How do you get your promotion in front of them? Are you going to use advertisements on a search engine or social media websites?

- What are their hobbies? What do they love to do already? What hobbies are they spending money on to do?
- What do they like to read? What genres do they like to read? Do they prefer audiobooks, printed books, magazines, or blogs?
- What do they like to eat? Are they vegan or do they love meat? Do they care about where the animals they eat come from?
- Are they healthy? Do they suffer from chronic illnesses?
- Are they married? Are they divorced? Are they in long-term relationships? Are they in homosexual or heterosexual relationships?
- Do they have children? How many? Are these children that they birthed? Are these children that they adopted? Do they have trouble conceiving?
- Are they homeowners? Or do they rent? What type of homes are they living in? Brownstones? Ranch homes?
- What type of interior décor is their style? Modern? Farmhouse? Contemporary? Chic?

- Do they travel? Do they travel domestically or internationally?
- Are they educated? If so, how much education do they have? What's the highest education they have?
- What do they do for a living? Are they blue-collar or white-collar workers?
- Do they have pets? Do they have dogs or cats? Or fish?
- What type of cars do they drive? Do they love luxury, hybrids, practical?
- What movies do they watch? What're their favorite genres?
- What TV shows do they watch? Are they watching cable or a paid service like Netflix or Hulu?

Forming a detailed profile and multiple profiles will help you to make connections with your target market in ways that you would not have done had you not been as detailed. Be as detailed as possible and look for connections. It will help you market to them as well. This step should not be taken lightly. Take the time to sit and think through this. You can give yourself a few hours in a room with a pen and paper or with your computer to take notes. Do not have any distractions. Do not turn the TV on, and you can even turn your phone off. Having a very focused, niche target demographic can be the difference between success and failure. You can mark it to more than one target demographic. However, you have to start with at least one target demographic first. Build on one target demographic, have success with that target demographic, and then move to the next target demographic. Next thing you know you will be selling to lots of people. Just remember that you have to crawl before you walk.

Ultimately, the brand for your company is something you should not stress about because companies rebrand all the time. Starting the company is more important than letting your brand stop you from getting started. If all else fails, just focus on what products you would buy or products you are interested in and build your business from there. You can then build your brand identities from there. These three brand identities are a great place to start, and it will help you research further and find out more about your customer. If you have the money for it, you can also hire a brand consultant to do the heavy lifting for you. If you have local business accelerators in your city or an SBA office or any nonprofit that helps economic development in the city, they may have workshops for developing your brand. So be sure to take advantage of these free opportunities to get feedback about your business. The next section will focus on answering all the tough questions many people have before they begin dropshipping.

The Downright Ugly

Dropshipping can be competitive, and there a few ugly things you must know before you begin.

- Profits margins can be low. You may think that the best products to sell are the ones that are expensive, but you may be surprised that some of the best products to sell are lower-priced items. This is not a hard and fast rule, but something you should keep in mind. Try to find a dropshipper that will let you get your product at the lowest price possible.
- Returns are inevitable. Most dropshipping businesses will have to deal with returns, so

you have to decide how you are going to handle them. You have to decide if you are going to offer no refunds, or accept returns and handle shipping, or any other policy you would like to create.

- You are not in control of shipping. Because you are not the supplier, you are not in control of shipping as if you were shipping the products yourself. This is something you should be aware and create protections through the shipping policies and return policies of your business. Under promise and overdeliver!
- Shipping can eat your profits, especially if you're doing worldwide shipping. You will want to negotiate and research to find the best deal with shipping. Sometimes using the USPS is the most efficient option, and they have pretty labels, so don't overlook them.
- Failure can be high. If you don't choose the right product, or pick the right website build or the right marketing option or any of the million reasons that must be right for your business to succeed, you will fail. The best way to overcome failure is to do lots of research

before you begin, monitor how much you are spending, and don't be afraid to make adjustments quickly. What you think may not always work, so don't be afraid to pivot if you see that something is not working.

Another Ugly Truth

Initially, you probably won't make much money. The first couple of months might not be profitable. However, if you can survive these first few months and begin to turn a profit, then you will be okay. You should keep detailed notes of your business sales and what you are making. For example, you can use an Excel spreadsheet to track your business expenses. Break down what everything will cost from shipping to what it costs to have your products manufactured to the packaging to the money you spent on advertisements. Keep it in a list. Then keep a daily count of how many sales you are making and what the orders are. That way you can see what products are most popular and reinvest in those products. You can also see if certain products are not making you any money.

Try to be as lean or spend as less as possible, then you can upgrade your business as you go. Try to make it out the first month so you can really start seeing a profit from what your orders are. Again, always reinvest your money back into the business and do things that work. So many people lose their business because they take too much money out.

If you see that you are not making as much money as you want initially, do not give up. Keep going. However, if you are burning through thousands of dollars every month, you may need to come up with a different strategy. And of course, everyone needs to have a point where they say I need to pivot before totally turning in the towel. Determine what the 'throwing in the towel' moment is for you. The most important thing is if something isn't working, learn from it and if you keep doing that you will find the winning strategy.

Answers to The Tough Questions

<u>If I don't have any money, how can I begin a dropshipping business?</u>

The great thing about dropshipping is that you don't have to have any money to get started. You can use a site like Zazzle or Teespring or another print-on-demand site and ask your friends and family to purchase a product from you there. Once you have enough money, you can then get fancier tools for your business. If your friends and family members have money, you can ask them for a loan or run a KickStarter or GoFundMe for your beginning expenses. Because dropshipping does not cost a lot to get started, you can find someone to help you out.

<u>What common mistakes should I look out for?</u>

Dropshipping can fail because people do not take the time to do the proper research before they get starting. Here are a few things you should do to help your business succeed.

- Take the extra time to look into the competition: Dropshipping has become competitive so make sure you are differentiating yourself from your competition. Looking at what your

competitors are doing is a great way to help you figure out how you will be different. Shopify has an entire marketplace you can look at to see what people are selling so you can compare notes.
- Do a test order from a supplier: Doing a test order will help you figure out how your supplier handles their orders. Some people avoid this step and have to pay the cost in the long-run. In the same vein, have a backup supplier that you should order from so you can always have a quality dropshipper around. Aliexpress and AliBaba aren't the only places you can find a dropshipper. Don't skimp on the research state of finding a great dropshipper or you will pay for it in the long run.

Should I focus on my passion or what will make me money?
This is a great question and one that is always asked no matter what business model someone wants to begin. If you can have a passion that is lucrative, that

is ideal. However, this question depends on your long-term goals. If you want to make money, you should focus on a product you know that will sell, and if you want to focus on your passion, find a product that will sell and you enjoy. These techniques will be explored more in Chapter 5.

How can I make sure that the quality of my dropshipping product is good?
You need to do a test order from your suppliers. Also, read the comments and look at the pictures that other people post. Having more than one quality dropshipper is imperative. Again, please do not skip on this step.

What should I be thinking about long-term for my dropshipping business?
One of the best pieces of advice is to think with the end if mind. Do you shouldsell your dropshipping business after a while? Do you shouldgive it to your children? Is this going to be a side business for you? Decide what your end goal is before you start building your dropshipping business so you can reach the goals and always have a big picture of what you need in mind. This will help you stay focused on your goals!

Great job on making it through this chapter! A lot of the principles covered in this chapter will help your dropshipping business start on the right foundation. Now that we have a strong foundation, we will move into the next concept of starting your dropshipping business which is to know about supplying and fulfilling.

Chapter 4: Supplying and Fulfilling: How It All Works

To be a successful dropshipper, you will have to fulfill orders. Order fulfillment is the process of receiving the orders that were placed on your website, packaging them and shipping them out to the customer. You can either do the fulfillment yourself, or you can hire an order fulfillment company to do it for you. There are pros and cons to each one. Your fulfillment needs will change over time so do not feel like you are locked into one method. The more orders you began to sell, the more the order fulfillment method will change to make sure that you are getting the most cost-effective deals. When you are using print-on-demand, the orders are filled by another company. So you do not ever have to touch the actual inventory. They handle everything for you. If you do not go to print-on-demand route, you have to fulfill the orders yourself. There are a few things you have to consider. There are different ways to do order fulfillment. You can also do a third-party order fulfillment meaning that you send your inventory to a third party, and they take care of the shipping for you.

The next way to tackle order fulfillment is by using a hybrid approach which combines a few different options. Before you begin selling, you have to map out a plan and go from there. Different processes are depending on which type of supplier you will use.

The dropshipping supply chain generally looks like this. You begin with the manufacturer then wholesalers then retailers who get the product to the consumer. When dropshipping, you shoulddeal directly with the manufacturer or wholesaler if you can to earn maximum profit. The manufacturer is the company that actually creates the product or products. Certain manufacturers already have a dropshipping program available so people like you can directly partner with them and sell the manufacturer's products. Working with the manufacturer is ideal because you get to cut out the middleman. You don't have to worry about other people dipping into your profits. If the manufacturer does not have a direct dropshipping program already, they may decide to deal with a wholesaler. A wholesaling business is one that buys products from the manufacturer at a wholesale price, and then resells the goods at a slightly higher price, but still at discounted wholesale price. Wholesalers may also be called distributors. Be aware that if you are buying your products from a wholesaler, you can get the price at a lower cost if you can strike a deal with the manufacturer. Some wholesalers like to deceive people and make it look like they are actually selling dropshipped items when they are not. You have to do your due diligence to make sure that you are getting the product at the cost as low as possible.

Order fulfillment is difficult because there are so many variables. It is difficult, but it is not impossible to do as long as you do your diligent research. As you are preparing to ship your items, you need to consider the most cost-effective ways to charge for shipping. In order to decide which manufacturer to use and make sure you're making maximum profit, you have to figure out your shipping options for your site. One of the easiest drivers for sales is to have free shipping on your website. With this option, the shipping is calculated into the price already. However, do not inflate your prices too much because this will cause a competitor to be more appealing to the customer. Some dropshipping owners do not even try to make money from shipping. They try to cut shipping costs and make their profits at the price of their products. It just depends on what you think is best. You can also just add to your product price the cost of shipping, so you at least break even with shipping. You definitely do not want to eat shipping costs. When you start reaching a higher volume of sales, your shipping costs can add up quickly. You do not want to go in debt just because you did not cover shipping properly.

Another shipping strategy is to have free shipping after a certain dollar amount. This ensures that the transaction that every customer is using is high enough to account for free shipping. Other companies have a flat free shipping rate. After you figure out the shipping options, you can then figure out which carrier will be the most cost effective to use. Deciding on who you use to ship is dependent upon cost versus reliability. You have to decide if you do not mind paying a little bit extra to make sure the package is delivered in a timely fashion or if you do not mind waiting a little bit longer. You will also have to consider if you shouldship internationally or not.

Oftentimes depending on what shipping carrier you use, once it leaves your hands, it is out of your control. The only thing you can do is refer them to the shipping company. However, you do need to think of a policy to address what's going to happen if packages get lost in the mail or if customers did not receive their packages. You have to decide what you think is fair and put that in the policy as well. Just like everything in this business, before you select a carrier make sure that you do plenty of research.

Another important part of order fulfillment is that you should consider where you will keep your inventory if you are not doing print-on-demand. If you have negotiated an awesome deal with the manufacturer for bulk pricing, you can also decide to store the inventory in a separate warehouse and ship from the warehouse. Mind you, if you do store the information in the separate warehouse, they may charge you a warehouse fee to store the product.

If you do not want to deal with any fulfillment responsibilities, you can hire a third-party fulfillment service. You just ship your discounted inventory to them, and then they charge you a processing fee to store, pack and ship your inventory. Make sure that you are aware of all the fees that are into taking into account when you use a fulfillment service and adjust your prices on your store accordingly. When you have done research, reach out to the fulfillment company and see what they do. You also want to see if they process returns or not. You can also ask questions to see how they handle heavy volume. You can see if they are willing to add your branding to packaging and if that will have an extra cost. You can also see if they have any experience shipping similar items. Then get the info to those companies and talk to them yourself. That way you can decide if you should go with that company or not.

Best Practices

You should investigate issues with shipping as soon as they occur. As soon as the customer reports that an issue happens with their package, you do the hard work to figure out what's going on. Take the matter into your own hands and make sure that the information was entered correctly and that you've done all that you can do and then report back promptly to the customer.

Be aware of international shipping issues as well as domestic shipping issues. The more you are prepared about what's going on, the better. This way people will not be confused about issues that may happen because of customs. Some people do not offer international shipping because it is just too difficult and they do not want the headache. This is something you should consider. However, just know that if you do not offer international shipping, you do leave some money on the table. Take the time to do the research upfront and to make maximum profit.

Take responsibility even if it is not your fault. This isn't always popular or fun, but people feel better if they know that someone is handling their issue. If you play the blame game, it does not leave a good taste in the customer's mouth or help them feel confident in your ability. When you are researching the carriers that you want to use, do not be afraid to ask about the insurance that they offer so you can offer that info to the customers.

Many businesses have relationships with different carriers depending on where they are going to ship their items. Smaller packages normally work better with the United States Postal Service, and they even have tracking. However, try to figure out which carrier is best for you, and try to take advantage of their discounts for being a loyal customer.

Let customers know that when they order the product by a certain time, the order will be shipped on the same day. If it is not ordered by a cut-off time, the order will be shipped the next day. This helps people that have an expectation of when their order will be delivered. It also creates a sense of urgency that can cause them to purchase sooner rather than later. Lastly, it gives you some breather time, so you do not feel pressured to always package products to ship.

As much as you can, try to let the customer know when their package is going to arrive. If you let them know ahead of time, they can expect it. However, make them aware of delays because of holidays or the weekends. Also, clearly specify the difference between a business day and a regular day. That way they won't be confused about when to expect their package. The more details you can give them, the better expectation the customer will have and the better experience they will have.

Always under-promise but over-deliver. People are not patient. So make sure you give plenty of time so they can check the shipping themselves. Also, give them a shipping number so they can check their tracking themselves without having to continue with login or contact you about information.

If you decide to do a fulfillment service, you can see if your fulfillment center also does customer service for order fulfillment to save you even more time. They may respond to customer's request about refunds or lost packages. See if they do that. If not, you may be able to negotiate this service. When you are looking into order fulfillment, definitely consider the customer service aspect. Customer service is one aspect that can make or break your brand. We all know brands that people hate to contact, and their sales suffer as a result. If a company is known for great customer service, they will often have loyal fans who do not mind paying whatever price they ask. Establish a culture of excellent customer service from the aspect, and you should be the person that starts that culture by your actions. As you grow, your employees will catch on and do the same.

Order fulfillment can be a headache if you are not organized. But once you figure out how to handle it. It is a piece of cake. You can play around with different systems until you figure out which one works best for you and your business. Whichever option you choose, try to keep costs as low as possible. Then you can upgrade to different options that are fancy once you bring in more profit. You do not want to kill your business with your shipping cost. This is a cost that cannot be avoided, but it does not have to eat all your profits. Successful dropshippers have fine-tuned their order fulfillment. They did not get through this process overnight, but they researched and fine-tuned the process for maximum efficiency. You can do the same!

Chapter 5: The Riches Are in the Niches: Choosing the Products You Will Sell

The purpose of this chapter is to help you figure out which niche you should sell your products in. There are two main strategies you can choose from - either creating a niche website based on your passion or creating a niche website based on profit potential - strictly. No matter what option you choose, there is a process you can follow to determine if a niche is a good one in which to start your business. It would be a shame for you to spend a lot of time building a website and then discover that you are not able to make any money from it. This chapter hopes to prevent that pain and heartbreak for you.

Before we get into the details, we will do a few definitions. A niche is a category or topic that describes the products that you will be selling. For example, a pet niche will sell items related to the pet. You narrow your niche down by becoming more specific. For example, in the pet niche, if you were to sell 'dog beds,' the niche would be narrower. To narrow dog beds, you would focus on selling 'dog beds for pit bulls.' The narrower your niche is, the easier it is to market to people in the niche. Thus, the niche would be considered macro-category. Niches consist of a keyword. The keyword in the niche is what people will search for when they are trying to buy products in your nice.

Here's a strategy to help you choose your niche and products to sell in your dropshipping store. Grab a piece of paper and jot down five problems people have, five fears people have and five topics that you are passionate about. From that list, choose the top 10 things that you are interested in selling. If you need a little bit more help, you can consider looking into topics around the following niches:

- Health – This niche encompasses so many topics. You can decide to try and tackle common illness or embarrassing illnesses like hemorrhoids or STD and find products around this topic that will help people.
- Teeth Whitening – This niche is evergreen because people always want to whiten their teeth. You can have different whitening products in your store and narrow the niche down based on whether if the products are vegan or not, etc.
- Yoga – This niche is popular amongst so many people whether they practice yoga for health reasons or spiritual reasons. There are a lot of accessories you can sell in this niche.
- Drones – The popularity of drones is just beginning. This is the perfect time to get in on this nice and create a site for the beginner or enthusiast. Drones also can be expensive and have lots of accessories so that you can make a lot of money in this niche
- Guns – People love their guns. This is a hot niche with lots of earning potential.

- Dating – Dating is a niche that you can help a lot of people. With communication always changing, this niche can definitely provide products to people in order to improve their love life.
- Décor – There is no doubt that the decor niche is a very popular niche with many offshoots you can choose from. With many rooms that you can decorate in a house to a different type of dwellings that you can decorate, there are plenty of products you can choose in this niche.
- Weight Loss or Weight Gain – Weight loss and weight gain is an illness that plagues many people. This niche is guaranteed to help you make money, especially if you can help people lose weight in an easy way, there is no way that you can't make money in this niche.
- Wedding – The wedding niche, no matter if you are targeting those who want a cheaper wedding or luxurious wedding, this is one niche in which you can't go wrong.
- Getting Pregnant – This is another great niche to target. There are lots of ways to approach this niche from the topics around sex

techniques to get the sex of the child that you want, to IVF options. This is one interesting niche for sure.

- Pet Niche – Who doesn't love their pet whether they are dogs, cats or other animals. This niche can focus on pet accessories or pet necessities in treating common illness. People love their pets and love to spend money on their pets, too.
- Survival – This is a popular niche because many people are preparing for the world's end and becoming more sufficient. This niche is all about helping people prepare whether it is building underground shelters, learning how to grow their own food or homesteading. This is an interesting niche that many more people are becoming interested in daily.
- Beauty – There is no way that you can't make money with this niche. Whether you are targeting hair, makeup, skin or clothes, the beauty niche always has trends you can discuss and money to be made.
- Nutrition – Nutrition is a popular niche because there are so many diets and diets one can write about. Nutrition is very popular, and

you can approach it from discussing foods, diets, kitchen gadgets, or even vitamins as starters, but the possibilities are really limitless.

- Baby Niche – Who doesn't love their babies, and who doesn't love spending money on babies? The baby niche can be approached from many angles from reviewing baby products to writing about the latest trends. This is a win-win niche for sure.

These are not every single niches that you can sell products in. This is just a list to help get your wheels turning. Once you have the list of niches you are interested in, it is now time to see if those topics will be profitable or not before deciding on your store.

Using Amazon is a great way to see how profitable a niche is. You simply go to Amazon.com and then look at the Amazon categories. Choose a category that you are interested in and then look at the sub-categories. Also, look for accessories that you could sell in this niche. Amazon is a great way to see if there are profitable products for your website because the entire world uses Amazon. Ideally, if your niche is one that people like to spend money in, you will be able to make money from the niche.

After narrowing your niche ideas down, you'll want to use Google to see if people are searching for information related to your niche next. Use the incognito search function so your web browsing history will not skew the results. Think of 10 terms that someone will type in when they are searching to buy something from your niche. When you look at the search results that come up, what type of websites pop up on the first page? Are they forums or branded websites? Are they small websites or authority websites? If you have lots of small websites, forums and Web 2.0 articles like Reddit or Squidoo. You may be able to rank for that site. Keep the list handy because we'll need it when trying to come up with product ideas. Keep a list of your results to stay organized and focused until you come up with a winner. Here's how to think about this process. When you are looking for something to buy, what terms do you use when typing into the Google box? Are you looking for reviews and testimonials or discounts and deals? A person searching for vacuums may not type in a specific word such as a name brand vacuum cleaner unless they know that's what they want. Search terms they may use could be 'cheapest vacuum to buy' or 'replacement bags for a vacuum.' These types of words show intent to buy. And you should try to use search terms like that to see what results Google gives you when you search for them or topics that show people intend to buy.

Once you have your niche ideas and product ideas, next, you should think of ways to brand the website. Are you able to create a brand around the website? Are you able to create a logo that promotes the site? Are you able to potentially sell the site to someone long-term? This will help you narrow down your niche topic even more. If you need help coming up with names for your website, you can use this resource: https://anadea.info/tools/online-business-name-generator. When you are thinking of a website name, try not to make it a direct search term that you may have found in your preliminary research. You do not want to name the website a keyword term because Google may overlook your site. Try to come up with a name that's related to your niche, but you can also brand it. For example, if we go back to the vacuum cleaner example, you do not want to use a specific vacuum cleaner as the website name. Perhaps VacuumBuyingGuide or VacuumPurchaseHelp will be better. You can let your creativity help you come up with a name that will show people who land on your site what your site is about.

Doing keyword research is important because it is the way to tell if people would be interested in your website or not. A keyword is simply the word that someone uses when they are searching for something on Google. A site tries to rank for a keyword, so when someone types that keyword into Google, their website comes up. Ideally, when ranking for a keyword, you should become the first step that pops up on Google. However, if you can be on the first page, that's helpful. Keyword research is the process of choosing words to rank for that will allow you to be the first page on Google. Selecting the right keywords will help more people find your site which means more money for you in the long run. Essentially good keywords can make or break your site, so it is important to find keywords that can help sustain your site.

There two types of keywords, long tail keywords and short tail keywords. Short tail keyword is something that's really broad like 'healthy diet' or 'kitchen appliances.' These are really difficult to try and rank for, but a long tail keyword contains at least three words and is highly specific to a solution your target audience is trying to solve. For example, a long tail keyword would be 'best vacuum for hardwood floors.' It is easier to rank for long-tail keywords because people who are entering these keywords are looking for solutions. This is important to do because you can be passionate about a topic, but if people are not searching for the topic, then you are not going to make money. This step allows you to really see if your niche can make money or not. We will want to use the Google Keyword Planner for this process and the Google search box itself. Paid tools you can use are Market Samurai and Long Tail Pro. For the beginner, focus more on understanding the process, and then you can decide if you should invest in pricy tools or not. We will now take some of the keywords that we used in our preliminary research to come up with a topic by using the free Google Keyword Planner Tool.

This is a free tool to use if you have a Gmail account. To access the tool, type in Google Keyword Planner and then sign in. The tool is free to use, so you do not have to pay for it; although Google may give you the impression that you have to order a campaign. Google wants you to buy something so the opening page can be a little aggressive, but there is a way to get around it. To get over the prompts when you sign in, follow these steps.

1. When you sign in, Google may ask a few questions about your main advertising goals, but click on the small letters in blue that say, 'Experienced with Google Ads?' so you can skip this step.
2. Then you will go to a page that asks about your campaign type. Select 'Create an account without a campaign' in blue under those boxes.
3. Then confirm your business info. This will take you to the main page.
4. In the top right corner, you should see your Gmail account info, but look to the left and select the Tools option. The very first panel on the left will be labeled 'Planning.'

5. Under 'Planning' there is the Keyword Planner, select the 'Keyword Planner.' You may have to select the 'Explore account' option first, which will then allow you to access the Keyword Planner.
6. Once you select the Keyword Planner option, you will then have the option to select two options: 'Find keywords' and 'Get search volume and forecasts.
7. You'll want to select the 'Find New keywords' option and make sure the US is selected as the target country. This means the number of people that search for that term monthly. This number will help you find keywords to rank for that are not that competitive but still can help you rank on Google.
8. Enter your search terms. You can enter multiple keywords or one at a time. Also try to find keywords that utilize question words such as how, what, why, etc. You will use these keywords in the product descriptions on your site.

Here are a few other search criterias you can use to help you find keywords to use on your website.

- Intent to Buy - Using your ideas for keywords, search for more keywords in the keyword tool that suggest the purchase will buy. Words can be 'discount,' 'coupon,' 'reviews' 'best' or 'quality.' Again, the easiest way is to think about what keywords you would type in before you buy something or if you are looking to purchase something.

- Cost Per Click - When you are entering keywords, a price shows up beside it. This price is what advertisers pay Google when someone types in that word and clicks on their ad. If the price is high, it shows that people are willing to pay big bucks for the keyword which signals it is a lucrative market.

- Trends - Another important thing to consider when choosing your keyword is the trends. Is the niche you want to sell products in a seasonal niche that happens only on certain holidays or is it an evergreen niche which means it can be sold all year long? It is good to have a combination of season and evergreen niches when you are more established, but

starting out; you may want to focus on evergreen niches.
- The Monthly Search Volume - When doing keyword research, try to find a keyword that has a volume from 800 to 5000 monthly searches and try to rank for the keyword. Now, this number may vary for some people. Some people want to look for keywords that are over 1000 searches a month up to 20,000 searches a month. As you get better with ranking your sites, you can choose this number for yourself; however, starting with 500 to 1000 monthly searches can help you rank faster and more easily than a higher volume number.

Another great tool to use is Google Trends. You can go to google.com/trends, and search for your niche and product ideas there. Google breaks down your keywords by month and monthly search volume so you can see if people are interested in your product or not.

Once you have your keywords, you should keep them because you will use them when you are creating your product listings on your website. This is called your on-site SEO. SEO stands for search engine optimization. This step makes sure that your keywords are in optimal places that will help you get on the first page of Google. You do not want to write your keywords in a way that isn't natural. You should try and keep it as natural as possible or use the keywords in your writing in a way that it makes sense. However, you do want to put your keywords in three key places. The first place to put your keyword is in your URL. Most sites allow you to modify the URL of your posts, so include your keyword in your URL. The next place you want the keyword to appear is in the meta- description. When you search for something in Google, the information under the website that pops up is called the meta- description. The last place you should put your keyword in is the description of your products. It is easy to get caught up in all the rules of SEO, but the most important thing to remember is that you optimize what you can. Using the keywords allows you to use Google to attract people to your website and set you apart from your competitors. You can have 1000s of sites that sell dog collars, but focusing on what types of dogs and why your collars are different in your product descriptions can help you sell more products. Don't fall into the trap of thinking that your lower prices are going to make you more competitive. You can still make a sizeable profit and still have a unique selling point that different from other businesses. When you are doing research, look at 5 competitors and note 5 things that you are doing differently. This helps you set yourself apart and makes your chances of succeeding stronger. You can even be more successful if you focus on how your product can solve people's problems when they purchase from you and no one else.

Having a specific niche will help you be more targeted in your marketing efforts, and this focus will help you to make more cells. Many people like to choose 18-65 as their target market, but that is just too broad. Try to break that market down and get as focused as possible. Remember the saying the riches are in the niches. When choosing your target demographic, also consider if you should work with the type of customers that buy those products. When you are selling you will have to engage customers at some point. Narrowing down your niche can be a long process, but it is important to go through the research to make sure that the niche is profitable. It would not be fun to do all the work of setting up the site for your niche, but realizing that there are not any profitable products that you can sell. So be sure to do your due diligence. Do not half-heartedly do this step. Once you have narrowed down your list of items, it is now time to think about looking for a dropshipper for your product.

Chapter 6: Supplier and Inventory 101

Finding a supplier and paying them for products is not as difficult as you may think. The key, like most of the steps in creating a dropshipping store, is to do your research upfront. This chapter will cover the basics of working with a supplier and managing your inventory.

Some things to consider when looking for a legitimate dropshipper is to see if they require an application or not. If a dropshipper is legitimate, they will have some sort of vetting process for you to access their low-cost products. They may even require that you have a reseller's license or an EIN number. (This information is covered in chapter 10.) Another indication that a dropshipper is legitimate is if they don't sell publicly. Most manufacturers and drop shippers like to deal with businesses directly. Real dropshippers also avoid letting people know what their prices are. So if you're doing research and you can't see the prices, this may be an indication that the dropshipper is legitimate. Lastly, some dropshippers have some of the worst looking websites ever. This is not necessarily a bad thing. This just shows that they are focusing on their business. This is not a hard-and-fast rule but don't be surprised or shocked or turned off if the website does not look as modern is it can be.

Here are some popular dropshipping manufactures and directories to begin with because of a variety of goods that they offer:
- SaleHoo
- AliExpress
- CollectiveFab
- TrendsGal
- Wholesale Central
- Doba
- MegaGoods
- InventorySource
- Dropshipper.com
- Your favorite business may have a dropshipping program. Do not be afraid to ask if they don't. You may work something out.

However, you can start here and keep researching until you find the product that you want to sell. Once you have found a supplier you want to work with, it's time to reach out to them directly by sending an introductory email. Using email will be the best way to find the suppliers that you want to work with as it will cut down your research time. If being able to speak to someone on the phone is important to you, just be sure that your supplier has your preferred mode of communication. Lots of suppliers, especially if they are overseas, use WhatsApp a lot so don't be alarmed if that is listed as a mode of communication.

When you reach out to the supplier, here are a few things to consider and ask about when making contact with the supplier.

- The first thing is to look at the product itself. Is the advertising copy on the product well-written? Are the graphics used to promote the product nice-looking? Would you purchase the product? Looking at how professional the product looks will help you see if you are going to make sales or not.
- Another important thing to know is how refunds are handled. This will help you understand how refunds can affect your return policy.

- You will ask them if you can use pictures of the products that they are using on their site, on your website.
- You will see if they have a product sample policy. Some require that you just order a product, others will send you a free product and you just pay for shipping.
- Can they customize labels for your business? Not everyone cares about this, but some people like to have a customizable feature. Even if a customer of yours was to see that labeling was from someone other than your business, you don't have to worry about that. Most people don't care as long as they get the product that they order.
- Can you get a different discount? There's nothing wrong with inquiring about a deeper discount up front. You can also inquire about future discounts based on the volume that you bring. If you can know that upfront, it will help you make more profit in the long run.
- How do you handle Chinese New Year? If you are dropshipping internationally and using manufacturers from China, inquire about this. When the Chinese New Year comes around,

sometimes manufacturers take weeks or months off at a time. Knowing how to deal with this will help you manage your workflow, so it's important to have multiple suppliers to choose from if necessary.

- Notice how the manufacturer responds to you. Are they prompt? Are they truthful? Sometimes when dealing with international manufacturers, they will tell a lie in order to remain polite. So make sure you are on the same page and that you and the manufacturer have a clear understanding of what you expect.
- Have they worked with other dropshippers? If so, can you speak with them or see references or reviews. I don't think there's anything wrong with reaching out to people who have done business with them. This will give you a more accurate description of what they have done.
- How do they handle being out of stock? This is a very important question to ask. It's best to have a backup supplier and then a site like Amazon to order and get to your customers if all else fails.

- How do you handle payment? Most dropshippers accepts credit cards and PayPal, but it's important to confirm. You will also want to see if they accept bulk orders or not. This will save you time. If they accept bulk orders, at the end of the day, you'll just send them the spreadsheet, and they'll fulfill the order instead of fulfilling the orders one-by-one yourself.

If you find a manufacturer with a dropshipping program, it does not matter if they are international or not, it's great to ask these questions so you can get a better understanding of how it would be to work with them. If they don't meet your needs, don't be afraid to go with a supplier who does. It's also important to have multiple suppliers. This will hedge you against issues concerning inventory running out and dealing with holiday breaks.

To manage your inventory, you can create a system using an Excel sheet and or pen and paper to figure out how to track your orders. Being organized and having separate SKUs for all your products and understanding how each of your suppliers' work is key to your dropshipping spaces. Thankfully, as dropshipping has advanced, there is lots of software in the eCommerce space that helps manage your order fulfillment. Oberlo is a popular order fulfillment software that many people use when dropshipping because it allows you to streamline the fulfillment process. Oberlo and other softwares like it allow you to see when the order was placed, if the order has been fulfilled, and if it has been shipped yet. Many of these softwares incorporate into e-commerce websites like Shopify or Big Cartel or even a WordPress site. If you do build your site from scratch, you can incorporate it into that website by using a certain code. Common order fulfillment software include ShipStation, EasyPost, Shippit, EasyShip - good for customers that do a lot of shipping internationally. If you can manage this order fulfillment in the digital space, it will help you in the long run. Setting up these processes initially will save you time and headaches in the end. Speaking of headaches, let's head to the next chapter which will discuss how to manage customer service in your dropshipping business.

Chapter 7: Easy Customer Service

Dropshipping is all about customer service. This is one of the key ways to distinguish your business from other businesses and to keep your customers coming back for purchase after purchase. This chapter will discuss how to deal with product returns, shipping issues, and best practices in customer service.

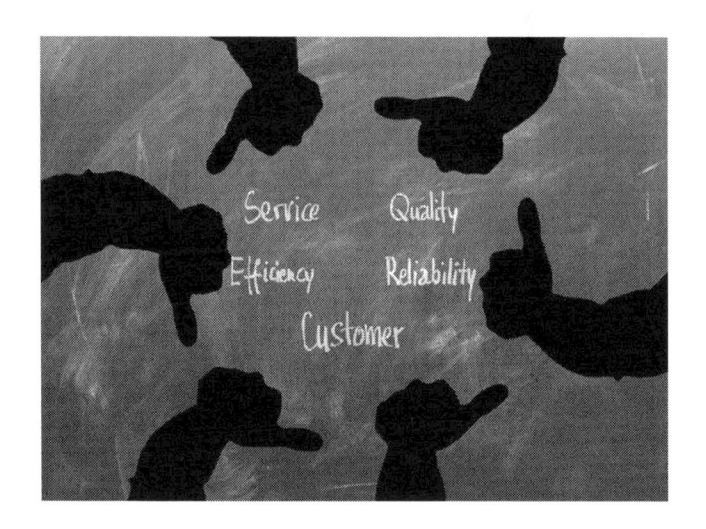

Product Returns 101

There are a few different options you can give a customer when dealing with products returns. When thinking about a product return policy, you will want to decide if you will offer returns or if you will not offer returns at all. Since you are trying to make money, try to have a customer service policy that optimizes every dollar before you have to issue a refund. When you look at your competition during the research phase, notice what their return policies are. Then you can adjust yours accordingly once you get into the habit of dealing with customers in your business.

Option 1: This return policy option is an easy option. You offer no returns at all. If you decide to choose this option, make sure that customers are aware of this policy and put it multiple times throughout your site.

Option 2: With this option, you send the customer a replacement product once they send their damaged product back. You can also ask for photo proof to make sure that customers are not trying to game you.

Option 3: You let the customer keep the damaged product and send a new one. This goes a long way in building rapport and loyalty with the customers, but only do this if you can afford it.

Option 4: You upgrade the customer to a different product in order to keep them happy. This is an example of going above and beyond your customer's expectations.

Option 5: You can give a discount on a different upgraded order.

These are a few options you can use when dealing with product return, but it's up to you to decide. Another great way to come up with a policy is to think about what you would like to happen if you were in your customer's shoes. However, remember your bottom line. Don't go out of business trying to do what's best for the customer. Your customer return policy has to make sense.

Shipping Issues

The key to handling any customer service issue is to manage the expectations of the customers. It doesn't matter if your supplier runs out of stock or if the customer does not get their order. The first thing you should do is apologize. This builds trust with the customer and shows that you are committed to solving their issue. Then you should let them know that you will do all that you can to help them solve their issue. Be prompt in the way you respond to them, and let them know that you will update them as soon as you find out. It's easy to blame issues on the supplier or the shipping carrier, but that makes you look like you're giving excuses for the issue. Take ownership of the issue and let the customer know that you are capable of solving the problem.

Customer service success in your dropshipping business is always about managing expectations. If you adhere to the under promise but over deliver ethos, your customers will always be happy. People hate to be ignored, and if you don't set expectations for your customers, they may think that you're being mean or evil. The best way to set expectations for your business is to have your policies clearly lined out and be transparent up front so customers won't be confused about things that are going on in your business. Once you have those procedures outlined in an easy-to-understand way, then it's time to go through the customer support process yourself. Take notes about what you can improve and then apply the policies. If you have your certain policies clearly outlined, the need for customers to contact you about every little thing will decrease dramatically.

One such policy is that you need to have is a FAQ section. This helps cut down the time people have to reach out to you because it gives them instant answers. Questions you should include in your frequently asked questions include:
- Where is my order?
- How do I return my order?
- When will you ship my order?
- How long does delivery take?
- General product questions.

If you notice that people continue to ask you the same questions, see if you can add them to the FAQs section. When customers reach out to you, see if you can automate the response emails or include a way for customers to track their order themselves. Automation is extremely helpful to your customer service effort. Freshdesk is a wonderful free platform you can use to manage your customer interactions, as well as regular autoresponders and using templates in your traditional email client.

Other pages you will want to have on your site, other than your FAQs include:

- About Us – This page explains what dropshipping site is about and how it can help them. It also gives a little info about the site's founder. This would be a great place to give insight into your shipping policy.
- Shipping Policy. This lets the site's visitors know how you are going to use their info. You can create a free one by going to freeprivacypolicy.com.
- Return Policy – Have a separate page to address it as well as including it in your FAQs gives your customers multiple ways to know about your return policy.
- Contact Us – This page is important because it legitimizes yourself and gives people lots of different ways to contact you. Include a physical address, which can be a virtual office, a phone number, which can be a free Google Voice number, an email address, and a contact form. There's nothing more frustrating than trying to reach someone and not having any way to contact them. If you are a one-person

operation, you may not want to have a phone number, and just want to be reached by mail. That is totally ok.

A great practice to have in your dropshipping business is a customer loyalty program. It helps to increase sales, build brand loyalty and it helps you get repeat customers. Once you have your email autoresponder setup you can create a program that rewards customers for buying from you a lot. This customer loyalty program is similar to big businesses in that they offer rewards when you use their business for multiple times. Other loyalty ideas you can have is the offer freebies for their birthdays and so many purchases.

Lastly, when thinking about your customer service ethos, you should encourage customers to interact with you. If you ask them for their thoughts, they don't mind sharing. They also don't mind sharing, especially if you offer any incentives for their information. The customers will let you know what you need to do to improve your business. Listen to them and adjust your customer service according.

Customer Service Best Practices

Overall, whether you are handling customer service or whether you outsource customer service, there are a few things you must keep in mind.

1.. You should handle customer returns as efficiently as possible. People love to brag on how well you took care of their order. Don't drop the ball or procrastinate on this because they can have negative long-term ramifications on your business. I'm sure you noticed that people always talk about the negative things of business did but hardly discuss the great things they did. To prevent this, don't give your customer something bad to talk about.

2. Empathize with your customers, listen to them, and build rapport. Listening to your customers and empathizing all plays a role in building rapport with your customers. I'm not sure if you've ever had a customer service experience with a customer service rep who does not care at all, but that sucks. If you truly want to find a solution to help your customers, they will notice. A major component empathizing with your customer is to always treat them with respect. You always want to keep in mind that without the

customer you would not have a business so make sure that you try to meet their needs. Apologize even if the fault isn't yours. Angry customers just want someone to let them know that they understand their frustration and that they apologize for the inconvenience.

3. As a business owner, it can be easy to forget the people that work for you. If you have employees, staff, or freelancers working for you, always be nice of them as well. They are your first customer. If they are happy to work for you, they will go above and beyond with your customers. You can never spoil your employees enough.

4. Follow up. Follow up. Follow up. Follow up on negative feedback and also follow up on sales. Thanking people for doing business with you goes a long way.

5. View customer service as a positive. It's easy to see customer service as a necessary evil, but if you treat customer service and the feedback it gives you as an important component to your business cannot live without, your business will thrive.

Here are a few customer service templates for the tough to help you get started. Let's face it. Interacting with happy customers is easy. The hard part is interacting with customers who are angry and unhappy.

<u>Template for Tough Situation</u>
<u>Template #1</u>
Dear (Customer),
I first would like to apologize that you are not having the best experience.

Your satisfaction and happiness are our number one priority. We are deeply sorry that it wasn't demonstrated to you.

We hate to see you go, and we definitely understand how this situation can upset you. We apologize for any inconvenience this may have caused.

All the best.

With Warm Regards
(Business Name)

Template #2

Dear (Customer),

We have processed your refund, and the amount should be in your bank account in the next few business days. Please note that a business day does not include the weekends or holidays.

I'm sorry that you didn't completely love your product. I understand how it cannot be for everyone. I hate to see you go.

If we can help find what you're looking for, please do not be afraid to reach out. I would like to give you insight into other options that we have and walk you through how this could be perfect for you. Thanks so much for trying us out.

I hope that our paths will cross again soon.

With Warm Regards,

(Customer support rep name)

Template #3

Dear (Customer),

I am saddened to hear that you have not received your order. This should not occur. I know how upsetting this can be, and I will relay this message to the appropriate department.

We are prioritizing your order, and our team is doing all we can to resolve the issue for you. I will let you know as soon as the issue is fixed.

Thank you for letting me know about your horrible experience. We want to make sure that every customer is happy. Again, I apologize for any inconvenience this may have caused you.

Please let me know if you have any concerns, comments or questions.

With Warm Regards,
(Customer support rep name)

Customer service is one of the most important aspects of building your business. If you do it well, you will know because your customers will keep coming back and bring others with them once they do.

Chapter 8: Marketing Your Dropshipping Business

Once your website in the process of being created, you will want to start marketing. You do not want to wait until your website is completely finished to start marketing. Marketing is the long-term process, and you can start building excitement for your dropshipping idea from the beginning to create more intense marketing buzz. You should get into the habit of doing a marketing every day. The sooner you can begin marketing, the better. This chapter will look at all of the ways you can market your dropshipping company. We will focus on social media, with an emphasis on social media, and guerilla marketing.

Instagram is going to be a very popular way to market your company since it is a visual-heavy social media platform. If you want to be taking seriously as a business, you definitely want to have an Instagram. Even if you have no experience with marketing, this chapter will help. One of the easiest ways to figure out how to market your brand is for you to look at other companies and see what they are doing. What does their Instagram look like? Are they using certain colors or are they focused more on stories? Are they just posting information without using color schemes or does it seem to have a method to their posting? It is important to think about what you want your imaging to look like on Instagram and make sure that it falls into your brand. You can begin marketing even if you do not have a name yet by engaging followers. You can ask them what's the best name that you can use for your business. You can also build engagement with your follower asking for their input about the colors you are going to use on the website or even logo designs. This will get people excited about what you are trying to do. When you finally have your brand assets, make sure that your logo is prominent on your Instagram page and have a link to your site and post your business' hashtag, as well.

The first place you should have a presence is Instagram. Instagram is important. You've got to have it. Instagram is probably the most important marketing platform for your brand in this era and one of the easiest to use. When you do start with Instagram, you can post pictures of your product with the models in a certain setting that compliments your brand. For example, if your vibe is laid back, you can have people chilling on the beach. If your brand sells baby clothes, what better way to show that than have cute pictures of cute babies in your clothes. Post pictures that feel they can see themselves in. Making your content relevant and engaging allows others to begin to really understand what your brand does it goes a long way towards building brand awareness.

When using Instagram, make sure you are using stories - a lot! You can use them to update followers on designs, new lines that you are launching, photoshoots, and behind the scenes content. Again, make sure that your stories are relevant to your brand and the brand niche. Instagram can take a lot of time, so be patient and be consistent. If anyone engages with you, make sure you comment back. Do not mind following people who say kind words or reposting people who are wearing your brand. Before you post always think about how it relates to your brand. Is your post helping your brand move forward or is it not focused on your branding at all? Be very specific with your brand vibe because this is how your customer will relate to you. McDonald's is not going to post anything about vegetables and vegan because that's not what their brand is. Make sure what your posting relates directly to your brand. Branding is the constant visual aesthetic of your business. So take your time in deciding what method you should use. Remember if something doesn't work do not be afraid to change it. It is not a deal-breaker to change your mind.

If you want to build your followers quickly, consider always running a promotion. This will keep people interested in your Instagram page. You can also consider running ads on Instagram. If you can afford $2 to $5 a day for Instagram advertisements, do it. When you sign up to business, they will walk you through the steps of creating your Instagram business account. When you are up and running, be mindful of what you're posting. You definitely do not want to post any random garbage. This can confuse the people who are fans of your brand as well as weaken your brand awareness.

You just do not want to post your products all the time, so it is important to switch up your posts. Try to change it up. If you run out of ideas or needs some ideas to help, here are a few Instagram ideas that you can post.

Behind the scene posts - People love to see what's going on behind the scenes. Behind the scene posts can show what your employees are doing or what you were doing to move the business forward like having meetings at a coffee shop. Behind the scenes posts show that you not just a corporation, but that you are someone that has a dream and that you are going for it. You can also be funny and genuine. People can tell if you are faking or not. Let your personality show so people can relate to you.

Volunteering posts or stories - There is nothing to tug at the heartstrings and the dollar strings than by posting ways that you are involved in the community. Show that your company is not just about profits. Show how you help out in the community. People will be interested in that and be willing to support.

Products use posts -- This is always fascinating. When people understand how the product is used, it makes the brand seems more personal, and it adds more brand awareness.

Cross-promotion of other brands – Cross-promotion of other brands may seem counterintuitive, but it can be a good idea. If your brand is really good for sitting in and writing in the coffee shop, why not partner with a coffee shop across the street? This way you both are promoted, and you form a relationship with another business in the process. When you made your brand identity, you created a lot of detailed questions about what your customer likes to do. Look at that brand identity questionnaire and then try to find connections that you can use with other brands.

Celebrating popular achievements – You have milestone posts that celebrate important achievements such as reaching 100 followers, or a thousand followers, or a million followers. You can also celebrate anything in between. Just be sure to show gratitude to your follower.

Giveaways - Giveaways are a fun way to engage your followers and get more followers. When you host a giveaway, make sure you have some type of incentive for the followers, whether they are tagging other people in your posts or using hashtags make sure that is getting your brand is getting out.

Discounts and promotions - Make sure that if you are offering promotions that they are in line with your business. You do not want to cut into your profit so do not underprice yourself. Some businesses do not offer discounts or promotions at all, and that's okay. You have to determine if you should offer them or not. Just do not underprice your brand if you do.

Quotes - Inspirational quotes are always a fun way to engage your followers and to get people to follow you. Think about quotes that describe your business or the aesthetic of your business and you can use them.

Sneak peeks -Giving people exclusive content about things that are coming to the forefront that has not been released is another way to engage your followers. They know that if they aren't following you on Instagram, they are going to be out the loop so surprise your followers every now and then.

Repost Your Followers -This is a popular one to use because you do not have to do anything. You can simply repost someone else's information and inspirational caption about why this relates to your brand. Or you can simply post someone who bought your products and looks good in it. If other people can see that others are wearing your brands, it goes a long way to show your brand's relevance.

Whether you're posting on Instagram or any social media, take advantage of hashtags, so people are able to follow you easily. Use hashtags that your followers are using and make sure you have your business-branded hashtag in all your posts. This is just a hashtag specific to your posts. Also, in your captions of all social media posts have your followers doing something in your caption. Try to encourage your followers to share your content so you can get more information out about your business. You can also share other simple actions to do. That way your marketing efforts will be compounded instead of just posting pretty pictures with no actions given. Some action words that are good to in captions are…

- Use our hashtag
- Tell a friend
- Tag a friend
- Tell us what you think
- Enter a giveaway.

Be observant and watch how other businesses are using their captions and hashtags, and do not be afraid to take inspiration from that.

Another way to get the word out about your brand is if you work with influencers on Instagram. You can decide to work with influencers that have Instagram accounts ranging from 1,000 to 9,000 followers. They would love to get free products, and to be put on your page if you have a good following. They also love to get products in exchange for a post about your brand but beware. You should make sure that they are not buying their followers. When you see someone that has a sizable following, look at their pictures and see if they have some type of engagement on their posts. Do they have comments and likes or are their posts blank? The more engaged their followers are, the more engaged they will be about the post about your posts which can result in more sales.

Instagram is just one aspect of your sales funnel. A sales funnel is what you used to guide people to make a purchase for you. For example, if you post something on Instagram, you ultimately drive them to your website to make a purchase. If you post a promotion on Instagram, you're guiding them down your funnel with the photo so they will buy from you. Sales is what matters at the end of the day so make sure the content you're posting is helping you make sales.

Instagram's sister company Facebook is also another valuable way to market your business. With over a billion people using the platform, you are sure to find someone to like your brand. Similar to Instagram you can come up with your social media posts. You can also connect your Facebook account to your Instagram account and whatever posts on your Instagram will also post on your Facebook automatically. If you do not have a lot of time, that will be the easiest route. However, if you have different content on different platforms, that diversifies your brand and make sure that people are tuned in with you on every social media platform. Facebook ads are also very effective. Similar to Instagram ads, you can run a $2 to $5 ad every day. Business.Facebook.com is the website to go to start your Facebook ads. Facebook ads are really easy to get off the ground, and there are lots of tutorials on YouTube that can show you how to use them. The main thing when using Facebook ads to make sure that you are advertising to people who you know will resonate with your brand. That way you are not wasting money attracting people that have no idea who you are.

You also will want to continue to find other brands, accounts, people that capture your brand's values or are similar to the vibe of your brand. Comment, follow and message them across all social media platforms. This will help you to build relationships and help your business thrive. You do not have to follow millions of people every day, but make a goal to maybe like, comment, or follow 5 people a day. Whatever you decide, be consistent, and you will watch your following grow. The more exposure you have, the better. So do not just limit yourself to Instagram or Facebook. You can use Pinterest, Tumblr, or whatever social media platform is best for you. However, you should separate your marketing efforts when you are evaluating where you get the most engagement. That way you can know which items are working for you and what things are not working for you. For example, if you noticed that most of your sales come from Instagram, you will want to spend more time on Instagram since that is bringing more sales for you. Anytime you have a sale; you can ask people where they heard about you. You will then realize where your marketing efforts are best spent.

When you decide what social media platforms you want to be on, it can be more than Instagram and Facebook; you will want to create a social media posting schedule. This helps you to stay organized, and have your content made in advance. It will also help you to outsource your social media posting to a virtual assistant if necessary. When you are creating the social media schedule, you can brainstorm different ideas of what you would like to post about. For example, every Monday it can be something related to your brand. Then on Tuesday maybe you can post people that are using your product. On Wednesday it can be another discount day. And you continue to create content every day until your social media is planned.

Depending on which platform you are using, you can find a way to upload posts in advance. That way the part work of posting is already done, and you just have to monitor and respond to the comment when the post goes out. Hootsuite and Buffer are popular software tools that allow you to schedule your posts in advance. If you need help managing your Instagram, you can look into bots and Instagram managing services. To create a professional-looking post, Canva is a great, free resource to use. With Canva, there are professional templates already created that you can edit to fit your colors. Then you just download the posts and then upload them.

You can even create posts from scratch if necessary. Every month evaluate the types of post that are popular and then create those posts over again. When you post about certain topics, you will see more likes and comments. If so, continue to post those types of posts. If you do not see any type of engagement for a certain post, you can consider changing what you post. The social media plan is not set in stone, and it is a way to make your life easier while you handle other aspects of your business. If you do decide to outsource this work to someone else, you can look at websites such as upwork.com or fiverr.com to find a virtual assistant that specializes in social media. Of course, the more you post on Instagram or any social media platform, the more engaged your followers will be. However, sometimes you do not have time to do that. So start off being consistent even if it is just one post a day and then grow from there. If you start off doing 10 posts a day, people are going to expect that. You can always start small and grow a little bit. That's where using bots and having assistance with your social media is helpful. You can also look for interns, like college students or relatives, who are looking to work with a growing brand to help manage your social media. Use what you have.

You also want to incorporate some form of email marketing. Ask for customer's emails in exchange for a discount coupon or a special gift if they sign up. That way when they sign up, you always have a way to tell people about your brand. Popular email marketing systems include MailChimp, which is free up to 2,000 people, and Aweber which has a month-long free trial. An email list is very important. In case Instagram was to ever shut down your account, you will still have the emails of people who are your followers, and you do not have to start from scratch. It is also important to have your own website, that way if Instagram shut you down you still have property where people engage with your brand. When you are running promotions on your social media, be sure that some of those promotions have incentives for people who give you their email. Another great and easy way to get people's emails is when you are launching your website. You can have a website in a countdown timer on your website and a place for them to give you your email when it launches. Having email is also important because you can send them reminder emails in case they were going to buy something from you but forgot. Shopify has this feature build in already.

Another important form of marketing that you can use is guerrilla marketing. Guerrilla marketing is using non-traditional marketing ways or more passive ways to help you sell your product. They are often low-cost as well and creative. One example guerrilla marketing is to have a sticker or other merchandise like lighters, grocery bags, pencils, or pens that have your branding design. That way when people see your brand, they may look it up. You can share this type of merch to make sure your brand is always advertised. Another effective way to advertise your business is through your email signature. Make sure you have your brand's information in your email signature, and that info will go out to everyone that you email. This helps them remember your brand. You also do not want to forget to ask your friends and family members to market for you. Most people will do it for free because they believe in you and your product. On the day of launch or even occasionally, you can get them to post on their social media or repost your post on your businesses Instagram page. That way information about your product is being spread by multiple people. To take this up a notch you can make a list of all your friends and family members that have a social media presence and then politely ask them to share information. Most people will love to do so. You can even stagger the times that they post so it won't be all at one time. This ensures that your information is being spread at different times in a strategic fashion. Additionally, you can take advantage of the direct sales method of selling and focus on the relationships that you have. You can decide to host a direct sales party. This way you are having fun and selling in a social setting. Most people do not mind coming to a party to buy. You can also add in perks for people who purchase a product before they get there. Add extra perks for those people who purchase more than one product. Of course, you should set the atmosphere with music and have food and drinks. Whatever you do, make sure that the party atmosphere matches your brand.

You also will want to join your local Chamber of Commerce. This step may cost a small fee, or it may not, but it is very effective. Tapping into your local market can help your business thrive. When you are a member of your chamber of commerce. They will do everything they can to see you succeed. They often have networking events and workshops that you can take advantage of that will help your business grow. If you are a minority, you will also want to consider joining the minority Chamber of Commerce in your city. Joining a Chamber of Commerce is the best-kept secret to starting your own online business. Everyone has to wear clothes, and they will be a great way to advertise your business through word-of-mouth. You also will be able to join a community of entrepreneurs that all have to deal with common business problems. You will be able to talk with them and figure out how to navigate issues that you are having that all businesses experience. Another way to find a community of entrepreneurs to connect with would be to use Craigslist, or social gathering sites like meetup.com. They often have entrepreneur groups that you can join. Some of these groups even require that you have referrals every month. If there is not such a gathering in your community, you may want to consider starting one. Starting a networking group will be a great way to spread the word about your business as well as forming a community of entrepreneurs.

There are a few other tips to keep in mind when marketing. You can have birthday promotions to reward people for being loyal to you. You can give them small gifts, coupons, or discounts. This goes a long way into building your brand awareness. You will also want to have a launch party. You can take footage of it and invite people. You can also send out press releases, so people know to come. And after you launch, remember to keep marketing. Do a little bit every day, so you are not overwhelmed. Come up with a name for people who use your products and create a Facebook group or address them on your Instagram posts. This helps people feel special, and soon everyone will want to wear what you are selling. You can also have gift guides all year long and describe cool ways to use your products. You can also post different blog posts to engage people while providing them with value. You also have to decide if you should buy followers or not. Instagram's policy is against buying followers, but many people do it anyway as a way to show that people are interested in their brand. If you do purchase such a service, you will want to erase the fake followers once you start getting real followers. Nothing will kill your credibility like people knowing that you buy your followers. Try to maintain your integrity and build your brand the hard way. This will pay off better in the long run.

To take your marketing efforts to another level, you can even think about hiring a sales representative. Sales are the lifeline of your both of your business, so if you have someone that is a master at sales, then you can definitely grow your business. However, you should make sure that the perks are worth it for the sales representative. Once you know how much money in advertisements that you had to spend in order to get a customer, you will know how to scale easily. You should make sure you are making a note of how many followers you have month by month so you can see your growth. You can also see if the growth with your followers is corresponding to sales. Remember, marketing is all about sales. You may be doing something that is fun and enjoyable with takes a lot of time but is resulting in no sales. In that case, you may want to pivot and refocus your efforts.

Just like every other aspect of your business as you are beginning your enterprise, you should find ways to keep costs low. Try to take advantage of word-of-mouth marketing and guerrilla marketing before you go into your paid options. However, do not be afraid of paid advertisements. It is an important part of your business. Start off small with your paid advertisements and then scale once an advertisement begins to get a lot of sales. As you are running your advertisements, continue to learn the best practices about advertisements and marketing. That way you can ensure that you are getting the most bang for your buck. Remember a lot of social media platforms change their algorithms often so make sure that you are staying up-to-date with the latest trends. Continue to research and learn about marketing. Similar to a lot of things in business, observation is one of the best tools you can use. Do not mind looking and swiping what works for other people. Once you add your own touch to it, the content will be brand-new. Use them as inspiration if you see a successful and watch the dollars come rolling in.

YouTube is a powerful tool you can use to drive traffic to your business. The great thing about YouTube videos is that it can help increase traffic to your website which means more sales and more profits for you. Most people do not take advantage of this awesome resource because they think you need to have a lot of views to use it, but you do not need a lot of views to make a lot of money. Just 1000 extra visits to your website is enough to make more money if you have your site optimized.

Just like using a niche website, the way for this YouTube strategy to work, you must have quality content on your YouTube page. People will not watch your videos if it is not addressing their problems. So make sure that the videos you create are high quality and address concerns related to your niche. You should aim for making about 10 videos initially, and then you can organize them in a playlist. This playlist is effective because once people watch one video, they may become addicted and watch more than one, which boosts views for your YouTube page and your website.

Similarly to when you optimize your website for SEO, you also want to optimize your videos for SEO. If you need to look up more keywords using the Google

Keyword Planner Tool, you can. Another easy way to figure out what keywords to use is to take advantage of Google's suggestion box. When you are trying to rank for a keyword, you should use Google. Google the keyword and see if a video appears in the search results when you Google it. If not, that's the keyword you should use in your video so your video can pop up when people Google the keyword. People love vides so using videos is an optimal way to direct people to your website. Once you have your keywords, it is important to optimize the keywords on the video itself.

- The first way to optimize your video is to use keywords in your title. You should make the title informative, but also helpful. Try to use the keyword naturally in the video to avoid being penalized by Google.
- The next place to optimize for keywords is in the description box. Take advantage of the description box and write long descriptions. However, divide the description into smaller paragraphs. You also want to have a link that is easily accessible to people above the fold that they can click on without having to extend the full description box. You can play around

with the description to figure out what type of description you prefer, but do not be afraid to write upwards to 200 to 300 words. Remember to add https:// before your link so it can become a clickable link. This step is important because people are lazy. If they cannot click on the link, they will not take the time to copy and paste the link and put it in the search bar. They just won't.

- Tags are the next place that you should optimize your keywords. Try to use about 10 to 12 tags per video that are related keywords.
- Also, take advantage of optimizing your thumbnail with an eye-catching thumbnail, and you can use a main keyword in the description there as well.

When you actually create the video, you should optimize the content in three important ways. The first way is to take advantage of overlays in the video. You can create overlays that direct people to your call to action which is the second way to optimize your video content. At the end of every video, give the viewer an instruction to do. You can use your overlay to direct them back to your site with the link included.

Tell people what to do so that they can do it. Additionally, when you create your website, encourage people to subscribe and like your channel. That way you have a built-in list that you can continue to market to.

Remember, when you set up your YouTube channel, do not forget out setting up your 'About' page. This helps people to learn more about you and know where to find you on all social media platforms. This helps people form a relationship with you on all your platforms. Also, do not be afraid to interact in the comments. People love interacting with YouTube creators. To really take your YouTube strategy to another level you can partner with other YouTubers in your niche. You guys can do videos together and share audiences. It is a definite win-win, but make sure you make it as easy as possible for the person you want to connect with.

Do not overlook the power of YouTube to grow your dropshipping. It is a great way to drive traffic to your site and bolster your asking price when you finally do sell your niche website! Most people do not take advantage of using YouTube. Do not be like those people. Just a few views can help you make more sales and increase your bottom line. When you sign up for YouTube, make sure that you optimize your page and have a well filled out 'About' page so people can find you outside of your YouTube channel. If nothing else, having a YouTube connected to your dropshipping can increase the asking price you ask if you were to ever sell the dropshipping one day. Do not leave that money on the table. Happy marketing your business!

Chapter 9: How to Scale Your Business

One reason why a dropshipping company does not start is that they are afraid of failure. Not just being afraid of failure, but a lot of people are afraid that their business will not be perfect from the offset. For some reason, people expect to be perfect the first time they do something. Remember that perfection is the enemy of progress. In the business sense, it's a lot better to be adequate at something than perfect. Expect that you are not going to be perfect at first. Having unrealistic expectations has stopped many people from taking the leap into owning their own business. Do not be like these people.

So what happens when you take action, and you begin to make money? You need to scale your business. You scale your business by putting more money into what's working. If you have an ad that is successful, put more money into that ad so you can make more money. If you have a product that sells really well, now it's time to buy more of that product to sell. If you notice that anything is bringing you in more profits, now is the time to put more money to bring even more profit.

Another way to scale your business is to target your business in different countries. You can outsource getting your store translated, and the ad that you run to being translated or you can focus on different countries that speak English. You will be amazed at how easy it is to target different markets and to bring in more money.

Another easy way to scale your business is to take advantage of your email list. When you have a list of customers who buy from you, you will always be able to scale. You can send out emails about new products to them. If you send out an email only once a month, consider sending out the email once a week. You can add different products, and you can offer upgrades. Sites like Shopify automate the ability you have to reach out to your customers. Take advantage of that! If you have an email list, don't waste your customers' time by sending out nonsense. Only send them the best information, and they will reward you with purchases.

Now that you're having money, you will also, want to consider outsourcing tasks that are not making you a lot of money. Some entrepreneurs spend so much time doing everything that they are not focusing on the tasks that bring in the most money. In this case, you will want to hire a virtual assistant to take care of tasks that you do not have time for or tasks that you do not enjoy doing. Fiverr is an excellent place to find low-cost virtual assistance. You can also Google virtual assistants from the Philippines or India for a low-cost virtual assistant that can help you with what you want to do. When you have located a virtual assistant that you may want to work with, you should communicate with them to see how you guys communicate. Then you will give them an initial task to see how they handle it. Once they handle according to your liking and you hire them for a book of hours, you can use an app like Slack or WhatsApp to communicate with them and make sure they are helping you with what you need. A virtual assistant will free up a lot of time for you. That way you can spend your time on more important things like making designs for your business, sending emails, and working on advertisements. Overall, be smart and grow your business. Take action, learn, and scale quickly.

Chapter 10: Other Considerations

Before you begin dropshipping, you need to consider a few things to help set you up for maximum success. When you are in the initial phase of starting your business, you should make sure that you have all the necessary business paperwork that you need so you will not be subjected to any financial trouble once your business becomes successful. This chapter will walk you through selecting your business name, getting your seller's permit, a wholesale license, and the easiest way to form your business when you are first beginning. These steps are going to require you to use your research skills. You will have to find some information on your own. It may be difficult especially if you have not done it before. However, the good thing is that these steps are free and there are a lot of resources you will be given in this chapter that can help you should you run into any trouble. Let's begin.

The first thing you should determine before you begin is what your name will be. You can use any type of method to come up with your name. Some people like to use their initials. Others use family names or names that have significance from important events in their life. Have fun! This is your business. However, keep in mind that your name can be a hindrance to people who will want to invest in your business. You should make sure that the name is professional and attractive enough that lenders will not mind lending to you if necessary. You also do not want to have a profane or offensive name that can prevent you from making sales further along the line. Ultimately you can take whatever route you want, but keeping the professionalism in a business name is advised. Once you have your name, you should make sure that is not trademarked by anyone else. The first thing you can do is to do a simple Google search of the name to see what pops up. You can also check your state's Secretary of State office to check for names of businesses in your state. To do so, Google 'Secretary of State business name search' and the name of your state. You can put your business name in the search bar and see if anything pops up. Then you will want to see if your name is already trademarked. You can visit the United States Patent and Trademark Office and do a quick search there. If there is another business with your name, do not fret. You still may be able to use the name. As long as there is not another business name trademarked in your state with the same name, you are free to use the name. If you are concerned about your business's name and want to have all the protection you can get, you may consider trademarking your business' name. It is an additional cost. It is not necessary in starting out, but some people like to have that protection. Oftentimes, people like to get started with the least amount necessary and then upgrade as their business makes more money.

After you get your business name, then you should figure out how to structure your business. Small businesses are often times structured differently from larger businesses. However, at any time you can always restructure your business. So do not feel pressured to have it one way. Oftentimes businesses change, so go ahead and get comfortable with constant changes. When deciding how to structure your business, you will want to consider if you should get started doing business as soon as possible or wait a little bit later to have everything structured a certain way before you begin. The easiest way to structure your business is by setting it up as a sole proprietorship. The sole proprietorship is technically not a legal entity. A sole proprietorship just means that the person who owns the business is responsible for its debt. A sole proprietor uses their own social security number as the business tax ID. A tax ID is important because it helps the government know who to contact about getting taxes when you make money. When you set your business up as a sole proprietorship, if something happens, like someone has an allergic reaction from your product, and they sue you, you will be responsible for battling the issue in court. Using your own social security for your business means that if your business suffers any financial setback and the business cannot pay from its profits, you will have to use your personal money to pay for the debt.

Some people do not feel comfortable using their own social security number to operate their business, so they use a different method. This method is similar to structuring their business as a sole proprietorship, but they just create a new tax ID for the business. The new tax ID is called an EIN. The EIN stands for Employer Identification Number (EIN), or the Federal Tax Identification Number. It is entirely free to procure. It can take a few weeks, anywhere from 4 to 5 weeks to get your EIN number. Once you get your EIN number, if this is the option you want to take, then you are able to apply for a seller's permit or a wholesale license. When you have your EIN number, you can still operate your business as a sole proprietor, but instead of using your social security number the business's tax ID will be the EIN number instead. The EIN number also gives you certain advantages that you can use when operating your business that a social security number does not. For example, if you have your EIN number, you are able to hire employees. You are also able to protect yourself from identity theft better. Some people like to structure their business as a sole proprietor because of ease of use. You can apply for your EIN, receive it and be good to go. If you are going to run everything on your own in your business, this may be the easiest way to get started.

However, another popular way that people like to use to structure their business is by creating an LLC. LLC means a limited liability company. They like the extra protection that an LLC provides. If you have an LLC, and your business is sued or falls into financial difficulty, you are not obligated to pay the debts from your personal assets. You are also protected from being sued for anything as your business would be responsible, not you, the sole proprietor. An LLC can be created online, using sites like Legal Zoom, and it can be created in any state that you would like to give your business better protections. No matter how you structure your business, many people like to use their home address as the place to set up their business. However, this isn't ideal because your information will be made known public and random people or debt collectors will have access to your information. Identity theft is real, so you should make sure that you are taking the proper precautions. There is nothing worse than thinking that it will not happen to you and it does. Prevent this from happening. Protect your information. When setting up your business, you may want to consider using a PO Box at your local post office, which is a small yearly fee, or using a virtual office, also a small monthly fee, that allows you use a different address than your regular address. Some people even rent a different house in order to use the house's address, but needless to say, that is an expensive option. Using a PO Box or virtual office is also helpful if you are trying to create your LLC in a different state. They just get the virtual office in the state that they want to create the LLC in and use the virtual address on the LLCs application. Certain states have better tax benefits for business and are popular to create an LLC in the state.

The top three states at the time of writing are Nevada, Wyoming, or Delaware. These places are typically more business-friendly and have limited income taxes. Delaware is popular because they do not tax out-of-state income. This means that if your business makes money outside of Delaware, you won't be taxed for it. Nevada is another popular destination to create an LLC because they do not tax business income, and they have a high level and anonymity in case the feds were ever to ask questions about your business. Wyoming is another popular place because they do not tax business income as well, and they have a higher level of anonymity than Nevada does. If you wanted to set up your LLC in one of these places, you could. It will be more expensive than a sole proprietorship. Also, the rules for LLCs change constantly depending on the state so you would be responsible for staying up-to-date on the state's rules. You would just research their rules on the states IRS or Secretary of State's office online. Some people like to start off as a sole proprietorship, and as they make more money, create the LLC. Some LLC's require that you pay a yearly fee. You would have to research to see what applies for that state. Popular places to format your LLC is only by doing it yourself if you feel comfortable finding all the information. Other people like to visit a lawyer's office and get their assistance. This may be expensive, but there are some lawyers that can help you for free if you visit your city's local Chamber of Commerce. They would be able to help you find lawyers who can help you pro bono. Other business structures are an S-Corp or C-corp, but these type of business structures are reserved for extremely large companies.

If you ever wanted to start the business with a friend, you can set it up as a partnership, which is similar to a sole proprietorship, but it is two or more people. You can get the EIN for the business, or you can even set it up as an LLC. You should set up your business properly from the beginning to avoid headaches later on. If you have the funds, you can probably set up as an LLC, but the ease of entry is going to be with the sole proprietorship or a partnership. At the very minimum, try to have an EIN number for your business, because of the added protection, and it is free.

There are also a few more differences you will want to consider when deciding to register your business as a sole proprietorship or an LLC. They are as follows:

- A sole proprietorship is cheaper to begin than an LLC. You do have to register the LLC in the state that your business is located in. You may have to pay an annual LLC filing fee depending on the state. An LLC also has to follow the state's bylaws pertaining to LLC conduct.
- An LLC requires that your business finances and business records are separate from your personal finances and records. This means that you have to have a separate banking account for your LLC. This requirement is not necessary for a sole proprietorship but is also

advised that you have a separate business account. That way you can keep your finances separate.
- An LLC required that you have a registered agent. A registered agent has to live in the state that you are registering your LLC in, and they are responsible for being able to receive all communications regarding your business. Some people like to use a registered agent company for this.
- When you have a sole proprietorship, you are taxed as a self-employed person. Whereas when you have an LLC, you can be taxed as a sole proprietor, partnership, or corporation.

When trying to decide how to register your business, you can also consult a lawyer or accountant for further questions. To save costs, try to visit a local law clinic at a university where you can get advice from local law students. They are a valuable resource to use when you are trying to find out legal questions for your business. You can also check out nonprofits in the area to see if they have pro bono lawyers that are willing to do work. There is lots of free legal advice everywhere you go. You just have to find it.

After you have your business structure, you can then apply for a sellers' permit. The seller's permit is important to have because it allows you to sell goods and products as a business. The seller's permit also allows you to collect sales tax for the products that you sell. It is important for you to collect sales tax because you have to pay those taxes quarterly to your state government. Lucky for you, a seller's permit is relatively easy to obtain. The place to obtain the seller's permit is going to vary state by state. The seller's permit may even vary city by city if you live in a very large state. How much sales tax you need to collect will also vary state by state. The easiest way to find where you need to get a seller's permit is to Google your city's name and sellers permit. Usually, the first link that opens is going to be the officer that you can go to and purchase your seller's permit.

Most seller's permits come as a temporary permit for selling at temporary events, like flea markets or fairs or pop-ups, or you can get a permanent seller's permit. If you want to make this a long-term business, make sure that you are filling out the application for a long-term seller's permit. Once you get the seller's permit printed off, fill it out. You can either return the seller's permit form by mail or in person. Make sure that you fill out all the information as correctly as possible to avoid any delays in getting your application processed. Another way to find the place where to get your seller's permit is to Google your state's name and 'Board of Equalization.' This will have the different regions of your state and the locations where to get your sales permit. It is important to know where to find their information because they can help you figure out where to find your local agency that can assist further. If you run into any issues, feel free to call the numbers or email them with any questions that you may have. The information they give you is free, and it is funded by taxpayers' dollars already so do not be shy to ask them. The service is already paid for. Another great resource for helping you find any permits you may need will be business.gov. This is a federal website that promotes small businesses in the country. They have other great resources for you to use. As a quick note, how long it takes to get your seller's permit can vary state by state so if you are in a rush, be sure to ask your local agency the processing time so you can make sure that you have everything in place before you begin selling. It is advisable that you do not start selling until you have your sales permit. That way you will not have to worry about any issues regarding your taxes. As another aside, you will also want to make sure that you have your sales taxes in order too if you are selling items online. You may even be responsible for sales tax on your website dependent on the state where the other person is buying from. When you are applying for your seller's permit, be sure to have the proper rates for sales and use taxes for your state. The attendants at the local agency will be able to help you. This information varies state-by-state, so make sure you have the right information for your state. Do not be afraid to ask questions! That will be the best way to make sure that all your questions are being answered and an easy way to navigate the process. It may feel overwhelming, but you can do it!

After you get your seller's permit, you may also need to get your wholesale license. This permit allows you to buy directly from distributors and manufacturers without having to pay retail sales tax so you can resell their products. By buying at a lower rate from a manufacturer or distributor, you will be able to make your price higher and make more profit. However, most of these businesses will not sell to you if you do not have a wholesale license. Depending on your state, the Board of Equalization may combine the seller's permit, and the wholesale license so be sure to ask them if you need to get a separate wholesale license when you are applying for your seller's permit. Again, research, research, research. It is integral to finding the right information.

As a heads up, this will be one of the longest, and potentially, most difficult aspects of starting your business. However, if you are able to overcome this obstacle it shows that you have what it takes on your own business. There is a lot of information out here about these types of services so take your time when trying to find out the information to make sure that is accurate. It is best to get started on these steps as soon as possible, so while you are waiting for your necessary documents, you can begin working on other aspects of your business.

The next way to handle your bookkeeping is to decide if you should hire somebody or keep up with your expenses yourself with a software like QuickBooks. Sometimes business resources like your SBA can offer bookkeeping help or even bookkeeping at a discount. Don't be afraid to reach out to these resources for help. Other important information you will need to keep for your business include payroll expenses and keeping up with your tax obligations. With your tax obligations, you'll also want to be sure to keep up with your tax deductions that you can possibly claim.

The Bank Account Issue

It is important to have a separate business account. SERIOUSLY. This will save you a lot of headache in the long run. Keep the money you make in that account and reinvest. Continue to reinvest the money in your bank account for as long as you can. Take off bank offers that want to attract new business customers. You can also see if you can get a PayPal business account that consists of extras perks. Also, smartly invest that money that you make. For example, if you have the chance to buy something in bulk, try to take advantage of that instead of doing something that you do not necessarily need at the moment. The only way to make money is to invest money. There is no getting without giving, so you are going to have to give something up. Once you have money to invest, try to buy more products or to upgrade your packaging or have a better website experience. Only you can determine the best use of money. Figure it out, and do that. Some people do not like to touch their money at all. They only reinvest if for a few months or years. You can set a goal to not spend the money until you reach a certain profit margin. Remember the name of the game is to keep costs low and sell high.

As a business owner, keep all your receipts for tax purposes. If you are going out to eat and discussing business, keep the receipt. Buying equipment for your business is another business expense. Services costs that you pay freelancers are also business expenses and can be used as a tax write-off. Other expenses you need to keep records of include electricity and internet, especially if you are working from a home office. Keep track of your cell phone bill or any expenses related to your business. Have the receipts and make sure you talk to your accountant. Having a good accountant is also ideal because if you are making over $10,000 every quarter, you will need to pay taxes. When you speak to your accountant, they will let you know the best way to make those payments. It sucks for you to have a lot of money, but then have to give that money up because of taxes. Stay on top of your tax obligations.

You also want to consider ways that you can save your money. Just because you have your own business does not mean that you cannot save your money. Your account will be able to position the best ways for you to save money and what accounts you can use as a self-employed person. One of the most popular ways to save money is to use a solo 401(K). This type of savings plan allows you to save up to $50,000 a year. You will also want to try to look into affordable medical costs. You can check out the Freelancers Union for some of the best medical insurance policies for self-employed people and business owners.

Don't Forget

Always keep in mind your exit strategy. Every business has an exit strategy which means how the business is going to end. Your business' exit strategy could be to sell the business, hire other people to run the business for you, or keep running yourself. At some point, you may get tired of running your business so it's good to know how it can go on without you before you even begin. Knowing what you should do with your business before you even begin can help you decide what type of business model you're going to choose.

The next thing you should consider before running your business is how other people can run it for you. A lot of people fail in their business because they try to do everything themselves. This helps them to wear themselves out easier. If you can think of how your business can run without you before you begin, this will help you survive your business long-term. One important aspect of running your business is to have processes. These processes help your business function and if you are clear about it, it is easy to explain to other people. Popular processes that you should keep in mind include customer service procedures, marketing procedures, sales procedures, bookkeeping, and social media management procedures to name a few. If you can get started with these procedures, then you will be on the right track.

Always consider how much time for family and other activities in your life do you need. A single person has much more time to devote to their business versus somebody who has a family. Having your own business is all about being well-rounded. You don't want to be chained in your office all day with no free time. Don't fall into the burnout trap. Asking these questions upfront can save you a lot of pain and heartache in the long run. Do the work upfront so you can be successful when things get tough with your business.

Know how you are defining your success. Once you have figured out what type of product you want to sell, you should think about what's going to make you successful. Why do you want your dropshipping business in the first place? Are you tired of the nine-to-five? Are you looking for financial freedom, are you looking for a career that's location-independent, whatever the reason for wanting to start a dropshipping is to think about what will make you successful dependent upon that reason? This is known as your why. Knowing why you should do this is going to be a central component to making sure that you survive this business journey.

Overall, be smart and grow your business. Your dropshipping business is able to succeed as long as you put the work into it. As you start to turn a profit, you can even craft your life to make sure that you are not letting your business consume you. Yes, you can have a business. Yes, you can have fun doing it, yes you can live your dreams. A business needs constant investment like a tree needs constant water. You have all the tools you need. Now get to watering!

Conclusion

Thank for making it through to the end of *Dropshipping: The Latest Strategies; Discover How to Make Money with Dropshipping*, let's hope it was informative and able to provide you with all of the tools you need to achieve your goals whatever they may be. Our conclusion will give a quick, big overview picture to get you started.

Dropshipping is a business model that does not require you to have any upfront inventory. Dropshipping is a simple process. You research products to decide what you want to dropship. Once you decide what you should sell, you find a company that does dropshipping for that particular product. When you decide what to sell, look at the company's prices and add your profit to the price. The total price will be the price that your customers pay you. After determining the price, you then create a website or ad and drive customers to the website with the ad. Once the customer places the order on your website, you then go back to the site that dropships the product and place the customer's order there. You pay the cost and pocket the profit. The dropshipping company then sends out the products to your customer from their warehouse, so you don't have to deal with the product at all. With just using a few clicks of a button, you get to keep the profit without the hassle of dealing with inventory or fulfilling orders.

Research skills are a must for this business model. You have to be willing to find drop shippers that dropship the product you want. Then you should check out the reviews of the company to see if other people have had favorable experiences with the company. Once you find the company you want to work with, then you are ready to take action. You also need to have writing skills for this business model. You'll need to be able to write copy on your website to describe what the product is. You also need to know how to write advertisements.

When people type phrases into the Google search bar, they are using keywords. Knowing how to find those keywords and use them to your advantage is at the heart of keyword research skills. Entering words into Google that your potential customers may use helps you see if the product you want to sell is something that people want to buy. Knowing that you have keywords that people are searching for will help you be successful. A great place to look for keywords is using the Google Keyword Planner, which is a free tool. SEO stands for search engine optimization, and these skills help you get your website on the first page of Google. Knowing how to properly use SEO can help you bring in more sales. There're certain places you can add keywords to give your website a boost. If you do not have SEO skills now, it is not a deal-breaker. You can slowly learn and optimize your website later.

Now for the good news. For the monetary investment, you don't need a lot of money. You can either use a website that is already up like Shopify or BigCartel, or you can create your own website and domain name for a few bucks. This business model does not require a lot of time to start up. You can spend four hours researching, or maybe less, to find a product that you want to drop ship. Once you figure out your product, you can set up your site, create a few ads, and you'll be ready to go.

Quick Guide to Get Started

1. Research the product that you want todropship. Find a product and make sure that the company is reputable and has great reviews about the quality of the product.
2. Create your website. Make sure your pictures look great. Some companies allow you to use the same pictures from there site. Others require that you use your own pictures of your websites. If this information is not clearly listed, you can ask the dropshipping company with their policy is about this. One of the best website creators to start is using Big Cartel or Shopify.
3. Be sure to have an email collector like AWeber or MailChimp so you can collect your customers' emails. You can offer a discount in exchange for your customers' emails. Once you have their emails, you can always advertise them. This step is simple to do by adding a few lines of code to your website.
4. Create an advertisement for your business and post it where customers can see it. You can use Facebook, YouTube, or other social media platforms to begin. Don't be afraid to tap into

your current network of family and friends to get your first sales.
5. Once you make your sales, you can invest in more advertising to promote your company more.

Pros and Cons

Pros

The pros of this business are that it does not cost a lot of money to start. You can utilize free tools so that you don't have to spend any money on websites or hosting.

Another pro of this type of business model is that you don't have to have a lot of money to get started. Since you don't have to have any inventory, you can quickly set up a website and focus on acquiring customers, which is the lifeline of any business. The key to any business is getting your first customer as soon as possible, then using the steps you used to get that first customer to get more customers.

This business model is great for people who have a lot of time but not a lot of money as a way to make money. Once they make money, they can use the profits to invest back into the business.

If you want to focus on print on demand items, like books or t-shirts or any other pain under my company's, you may need to have additional skills such as graphic designing or writing. Popular print-on-demand websites include teespring.com, Zazzle and printful.com.

Cons

Choosing the right product to sell is very important when trying to decide what you should sell. In order to be successful, you have to make sales. If you choose a very competitive niche, it can take a while in order to sell products. Therefore, you should make sure your branding is different than other companies to set yourself apart from your competitors.

If you decide to jump right into paid advertising, you may lose money if you aren't able to make customers quickly. If you are cash-strapped, you should rely more on word-of-mouth advertising to make a few sales, and then use that money to invest in paid advertising.

Why People Fail

People fail with dropshipping because they give up too soon, and don't adjust their marketing strategies fast enough. If you're in a competitive niche, you may want to give yourself a week or two to see if any sales come in. If none come in, then adjust your strategy.

To help you reach your success faster. I want to go over a few concepts that could hinder you from taking action. If you're aware of these hindrances, when it happens to you, you won't be fooled by them. The first hindrance is you don't want to take action because you're afraid of failure. Yes, you're taking action by reading this book, but it does not end here. Do not be afraid to take action, and do not be afraid of failure. I'm here to tell you today that failure is a part of the business process. Business owners fail a lot, but it's not the failure that's important. It's the information they learn from the failure that helps them to make adjustments to their business quickly. That's why it's so important to begin as soon as you know what you want. This ensures that you can gather information quickly, and it is that information that helps your business be successful. If you're running an ad and you don't get any responses on it, don't be afraid to try a different ad. As soon as you know something isn't working, try something else. Using this simple concept of learning from failures quickly will help your business survive long-term.

Now that you understand what you need, the next step is to get started! Get to researching so you can figure out the best product for you sell! The ball is in your court, and it's up to you to decide how successful you want to be. Finally, if you found this book useful in any way, a review on Amazon is always appreciated!

Printed in Poland
by Amazon Fulfillment
Poland Sp. z o.o., Wrocław